THE LION
Storyteller
BIBLE

Retold by Bob Hartman
Illustrations by Krisztina Kállai Nagy

LION
CHILDREN'S

With love to my grandson Malachi   B.H.

With love to my daughter, Bori –
may you enjoy and grow to
understand these stories   K.K.N.

Text copyright © 2008 Bob Hartman
Illustrations copyright © 2008 Krisztina Kállai Nagy
This edition copyright © 2008 Lion Hudson

The moral rights of the author and illustrator
have been asserted

A Lion Children's Book
an imprint of
Lion Hudson plc
Wilkinson House, Jordan Hill Road,
Oxford OX2 8DR, England
www.lionhudson.com
ISBN: 978-0-7459-4980-2

First edition 2008
10 9 8 7 6 5 4 3 2 1 0

Some of the stories in this book were first published as
The Lion Storyteller Bible in 1995.
This expanded edition first published in 2008.

A catalogue record for this book is available
from the British Library

Typeset in 13/16 Century Schoolbook BT
Printed and bound in Singapore

Contents

Introduction 6

The Old Testament

In the Beginning 8
The story of creation: Genesis 1–2

A Sad Day 10
The story of the fall: Genesis 3

A Special Promise 12
The story of Noah: Genesis 6–9

The Tall Tower 14
The story of the Tower of Babel: Genesis 11

God's Friend 16
The call of Abraham: Genesis 12, 17–18, 21

The Bad Brother 18
The story of Jacob and Esau: Genesis 27

The Runaway 20
The story of Jacob and Laban:
Genesis 28–29, 33

Joseph the Dreamer 22
The story of the young Joseph: Genesis 37

Joseph the Prisoner 24
The story of Joseph and the king's dreams:
Genesis 39–41

Joseph the Ruler 26
The story of Joseph in Egypt: Genesis 42–45

The Secret Baby 28
The birth of Moses: Exodus 1–2

The Burning Bush 30
The call of Moses: Exodus 3–4

The Great Escape 32
The story of the exodus: Exodus 7–14

A Long Journey 34
Moses leads his people through the
wilderness: Exodus 16–40

Spies in Canaan 36
Entering the Promised Land:
Numbers 13–14, Deuteronomy 1

The Walls Fall Down 38
The battle of Jericho: Joshua 6

A Brave and Mighty Man 40
The story of Gideon: Judges 6–7

Samson's Great Deeds 42
Tales of a strong man: Judges 14–16

Samson and Delilah 44
A story of betrayal: Judges 16

Samson and the Philistines 46
Samson's last act: Judges 16

Ruth Finds a New Home 48
The story of a foreigner: Ruth 1–4

Samuel Hears a Voice 50
The call of Samuel: 1 Samuel 3

Samuel the Kingmaker 52
Samuel chooses Israel's king: 1 Samuel 8–16

David the Giant-Killer 54
The story of David and Goliath: 1 Samuel 17

The Wise King 56
The wisdom of Solomon: 1 Kings 3

Elijah and the Ravens 58
Elijah in hiding: 1 Kings 16–17

A Jar and a Jug 60
Elijah and the widow: 1 Kings 17

God Sends Fire 62
Elijah and the prophets of Baal: 1 Kings 18

The Helpful Servant 64
The story of Naaman: 2 Kings 5

Jonah the Groaner 66
The story of Jonah: Jonah

Hezekiah Trusts God 68
A miracle of healing: 2 Kings 20,
2 Chronicles 32, Isaiah 38

Down in the Well 70
The story of Jeremiah: Jeremiah 38

The Boys Who Liked to Say No 72
Four boys who kept God's rules: Daniel 1

The Men Who Liked to Say No 74
The story of the fiery furnace: Daniel 3

Daniel and the Lions 76
Daniel in the lions' den: Daniel 6

Esther Was a Star 78
A Jewish girl saves her people: Esther 2–9

A Time to Build 80
Rebuilding Jerusalem: Nehemiah 1–4

The New Testament

The First Christmas 84
The birth of Jesus: Matthew 1, Luke 1–2

The Wise Men's Visit 86
The story of the wise men: Matthew 2

The Boy in the Temple 88
The visit to the Temple: Luke 2

Jesus is Baptized 90
The baptism of Jesus: Matthew 3, Mark 1,
Luke 3, John 1

Jesus' Special Friends 92
Jesus calls the first disciples: Luke 5

Down Through the Roof 94
Jesus heals a paralysed man: Luke 5

The Centurion's Servant 96
Jesus heals a Roman's servant: Luke 7

The Storm on the Lake 98
Jesus calms the wind and waves: Matthew 8,
Mark 4, Luke 8

'Time to Get Up' 100
The story of Jairus' daughter: Matthew 9,
Mark 5, Luke 8

The Marvellous Picnic 102
Jesus feeds five thousand people: Matthew 14,
Mark 6, Luke 9

The Kind Stranger 104
The story of the good Samaritan: Luke 10

The Two Sisters 106
Jesus visits Mary and Martha: Luke 10

The Unforgiving Servant 108
Jesus' story about forgiveness: Matthew 18

'I Can See!' 110
Jesus heals a blind man: John 9

The Two Houses 112
The parable of the two builders: Matthew 7, Luke 6

The Big Party 114
The parable of the great feast: Matthew 22, Luke 14

The Good Shepherd 116
The parable of the lost sheep: Matthew 18, Luke 15

The Lost Coin 118
The parable of the lost coin: Luke 15

The Big Spender 120
The parable of the lost son: Luke 15

Big Bags of Money 122
The parable of the talents: Matthew 25

The Man Who Came Back 124
Jesus heals ten men: Luke 17

The Pharisee and the Tax Collector 126
Jesus' story about heartfelt prayer: Luke 18

Jesus and the Children 128
Jesus blesses little children: Matthew 19, Mark 10, Luke 18

Jesus and the Taxman 130
Jesus and Zacchaeus: Luke 19

The Great Parade 132
The story of Palm Sunday: Matthew 21, Mark 11, Luke 19, John 12

The Widow's Coins 134
Jesus' story about giving: Mark 12, Luke 21

An Important Meal 136
The last supper and a betrayal: Matthew 26, Mark 14, Luke 22, John 13

A Dreadful Day 138
The story of Good Friday: Matthew 27, Mark 15, Luke 23, John 19

A Happy Day 140
The story of Easter: Matthew 28, Mark 16, Luke 24, John 20

On the Road to Emmaus 142
A resurrection appearance: Luke 24

Goodbye at Last 144
Jesus appears to his friends: Matthew 28, Mark 16, Luke 24, John 21

The Helper Arrives 146
Pentecost: Acts 2

The Beautiful Gate 148
Peter and John heal a lame man: Acts 3

On the Road to Damascus 150
Paul's conversion: Acts 7–9

Tabitha Wakes Up 152
Peter heals a good woman: Acts 9

The Earth Shakes 154
Paul and Silas in prison: Acts 16

Paul is Shipwrecked 156
Paul goes to Rome: Acts 2–21, 27–28

Sharing stories with a crowd 158

Introduction: As a pastor, parent and children's author, I realize that there are already many children's Bibles available. So I want to tell you what makes the *Lion Storyteller Bible* special. And I want to share with you several hopes I have for this book.

First, I hope that it will bring you closer to the children in your life. This book is meant to be read aloud – shared with an audience of children or grandchildren, with a class at school or a church children's group. That's how many of the Bible stories were handed down in the first place: shouted by prophets, proclaimed by preachers, whispered as prayers – spoken out loud by one person to another. People were brought together by those words. They asked questions, shared insights or simply wondered together at God's love and power.

Next, I hope this book will help you to become a better storyteller. I've been telling stories professionally for over twenty years, and I am always amazed by the power of a story well told to capture and entertain and delight. I rewrote the Bible stories in this book not so much to be read as to be told. I worked hard to be faithful to the original narrative, but I also included some storytelling devices – repetition, rhythm and wordplay – so that the stories would land well on the listening ear.

What remains is for you, the storyteller, to supply the voice. And so I encourage you to familiarize yourself with the stories before you read them out loud. Discover the theme-threads I have woven to tie each story together. Make up different voices for the characters. Come up with some noises or actions of your own. And if you'd like some ideas on how to do that, you might find it helpful to look at the notes at the back of the book. There you will find suggested actions and storytelling tips for each of the stories in this collection. But above all, have fun! For that is the best guarantee that your children will enjoy these stories too.

Finally, a story Bible, by its very nature, requires the selection of certain stories and the omission of others. In this case, the stories have been chosen because they show, in terms young children will understand, that God is love. My hope, as a Christian, is that, having seen God in these stories, your children will learn to trust God and to listen for God's voice. And to love God in return.

Bob Hartman

Stories from
The Old Testament

In the Beginning

At first, there wasn't anything at all. Nothing! So God set to work. But he didn't use his hands or a special machine. He spoke, that's all. He said, 'I'd like some light.' And there was light. Brighter than a summer morning or a thousand Christmas candles.

God spoke again. He said, 'Sky. I'd like some sky. And some water underneath.' And, sure enough, there it was. The bright blue sky. With the dark blue heavens above it. And the blue-green sea below.

'Earth.' That's what God said next, hard and firm, as if he really meant it. And the blue-green waters parted, and there was dry land underneath. Great patches of it, dirt black and brown. Here and there, all over the world.

'We need some colour,' God whispered, as if he were thinking out loud. And, quivering with excitement, green growing things crept right up out of the dark earth, then burst into blossom – red, orange and blue! Pine trees and palm trees. Rose bushes and blackberry bushes. Tulips and chrysanthemums.

God shouted next.

'Day – shining sun!'

'Night – shining moon!'

'Bright shining stars!'

And there they were, for morning and evening, summer and winter – time and heat and light!

After that, God called to the sky, as if he were expecting some kind of an answer.

'Come forth, flying things!' he cried.

And through the clouds
they came. Flying high and flying low.
Flying large and flying small. Eagles and insects.
Hummingbirds and hawks.

Then God called to the sea.

'Come forth, splashing things!'

And they came to him too, leaping right up through the waves.
Sailfish and swordfish. Dolphins and trout. Great grinning
humpback whales.

Finally, God called to the earth.

'Come forth, walking things, crawling things, running,
hopping, climbing things!'

And sure enough, they came. Up from burrows. Down
from trees. Out of the high grass, and across the open
plains.

Now everything was ready. Good and ready. So God
spoke again.

'Man and woman,' is what he said, as if he were calling
the names of his very best friends.

And out of the dust came Adam and Eve. To enjoy all
that God had made. To take care of it for him. And to
talk with him.

'This is the way things ought to be,' God said at
last. 'This is what I call good!'

A Sad Day

'Welcome to my world!' God said to Adam. 'It's good, isn't it?'

'Welcome to my garden!' God said to Eve. 'This is the most beautiful place of all. And I want it to be your home. Take care of the animals for me. Take care of the plants. And eat whatever you like. There are plenty of trees to pick from.'

Adam and Eve didn't know what to say. They looked at the garden. They looked at each other. And then they smiled the world's first smile.

Life was going to be perfect here. Just perfect.

'There's just one more thing,' God said. 'Do you see that tree over there? The one in the middle of the garden? Well, the fruit on that tree is not good for you. If you eat it, you will make me very unhappy. And you will have to leave this beautiful place.'

Adam and Eve looked at each other again. With so many trees to choose from, that hardly seemed to be a problem. And for a long time, they were content with soft juicy pears, sweet thick-skinned oranges and round ripe melons.

Then, one day, the serpent came to visit.

'Tell me,' the serpent said to Eve, 'which trees are you allowed to eat from?'

'Every tree!' Eve smiled. 'Except the one in the middle of the garden.'

'Oh?' said the crafty serpent.

'And why is that?'

10

'Because it would make God unhappy,' Eve answered. 'And we would have to leave this beautiful place.'

'Ridiculous!' laughed the serpent. 'God does not want you to eat that fruit because he knows it would make you as clever as him. You know all about being good. But God has told you nothing about what it means to be bad. Eat the fruit and you will know all about that too!'

Eve thought that the fruit looked delicious. She had sometimes wondered what it tasted like. And it wasn't really fair of God to keep things from them.

So she picked a piece. And took a bite. And gave Adam a taste as well.

And right away, they discovered what it meant to do something bad. Their stomachs churned with guilt. Their faces turned red with shame. And instead of running to meet God when he next visited the garden, they ran away to hide.

'I know what you have done,' God called out sadly. 'Now you will have to leave this beautiful place.'

'Goodbye,' God said to Adam. 'From now on, you will have to scratch at the earth for the food you eat.'

'Goodbye,' God said to Eve. 'Your life will be hard too.'

'And when your lives end,' God said finally, 'you will go back to the ground from which you came.'

Adam and Eve looked at each other. Then they walked sadly out of the garden. They had learned what it meant to be bad. And they had changed God's good world forever.

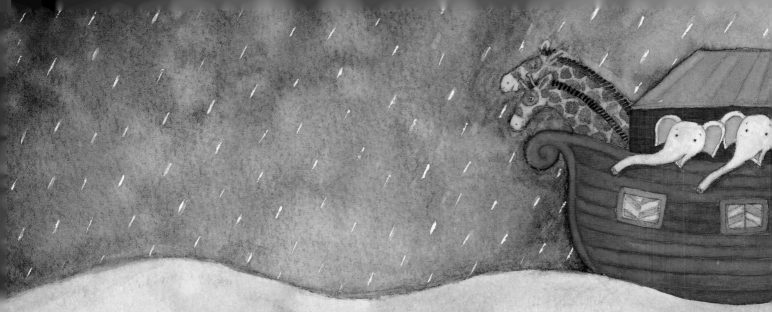

A Special Promise

God was sad. Very sad. Everywhere he looked, he saw people making bad choices. Hating each other. Hurting each other. Making a mess of his beautiful world.

'I need to start all over again,' God decided. 'I need to make my world clean.' And that's when he talked to Noah.

Noah was not like the rest. He was a good man and God knew it. So God told him to build a boat. A boat big enough to hold:

Noah,

his wife,

his three sons,

their wives,

a pair of every animal in the world,

and food enough to feed all of them for a very long time!

Noah's family was surprised when he told them what he was going to do.

Noah's neighbours thought it strange of him to build a boat so far from the sea.

And it wasn't easy chasing, and catching, and cleaning up after all those animals.

But Noah was a good man. He did what God told him – even when it was hard.

At last, when they were all tucked safely away in the boat, God shut the door. And then it started to rain.

It rained for forty days.

It rained for forty nights.

It rained harder than Noah had ever seen it rain before.

It rained so hard that the streams, and the rivers, and even the seas burst their banks and shores and began to flood. Soon every sandy beach, every rocky path, every patch of muddy earth had disappeared beneath the water.

And the boat began to float.

It floated above the houses. It floated above the trees. It floated above the hills, and then above the mountains too.

It floated for days and weeks and months.

And then it stopped: stuck at the top of a tall mountain.

Noah opened a window to look out. The water was going down, but the world was far from dry.

So he sent out a dove. And when the dove did not come back, Noah knew that it had found a dry place to build its nest.

'Come out!' God called finally. 'Come out of the boat! The world is dry. The world is clean. And now you and your family and all the animals must have children and fill it full of life again!'

'Hooray!' Noah celebrated. And he thanked God for saving him.

God was happy too. So he painted the world's first rainbow in the sky – to celebrate his fresh, clean world. And to promise that he would never send a flood like that again.

The Tall Tower

God looked. Something was happening in the land of
   Shinar.

God listened. And this is what he heard:

'Hey, you,' called a tall man. 'Throw me a brick.'

'Here you go,' snorted a short man, 'and could you
pass me that axe?'

From all over the world, they had come – tall people,
short people, fat people, thin people, all kinds of people.
And they were building a tower!

Up, up, up they went. Stirring mortar. Making bricks.
And hauling them high into the sky.

It was a big job. It was hard work. So it was a good thing
they all spoke the same language – at least they could
understand each other.

God looked and God listened again. This is what he
heard:

'Say,' asked a fat man, 'why are we building this tower
anyway?'

'It's simple,' grinned a thin man. 'When we are finished
this will be the tallest tower in the whole world.

'People will pass by, look at it and be amazed. We'll be
more famous than the greatest king. We'll be more important
than God himself!'

Now when God heard that, he jumped! And then he
smiled.

'More important than me?' he chuckled. 'We'll see
about that.'

That's when God decided to play the world's first trick.
Did he wave his hand? Did he say some special words?

14

Or did he just think it into happening? No one knows.
But the next time God listened, this is what he heard:
    'Hey, you,' called the tall man, 'pass me some
mortar.'
    'Fortwort?' snorted the short man. 'Hort
mort a bortle.' (Which means something like,
'What did you say? I can't understand you.')
    God chuckled again. He was enjoying this. So he
listened some more.
    'Excuse me,' asked the fat man, 'could I borrow your
hammer?'
    But the thin man didn't have a clue what he meant.
'Hub-wub?' he asked. 'Flub-bub-a-gubble.' (Which
means something like, 'What? You're not making sense.')
    And so it was, all over the tower. Instead of one
language, there were suddenly hundreds. The workers
couldn't understand each other. How could they go on?
    So down, down, down they climbed, dropping their tools
as they went. Then they babbled off in every direction,
leaving the tower half-finished, half-done.
    And whenever people passed by they were not amazed.
No: some sniggered, some pointed and some even said,
'Flep-nepp, shlepp-rep-a-zepp.' (Which means something
like, 'See, those men weren't more important than God
after all.')

God's Friend

Abraham was rich. He had lots of servants to do his work for him. He had lots of camels and sheep. And he lived with his wife in a very nice place called Haran.

One day, God spoke to Abraham.

'I want you to leave Haran,' he said. 'Because I have a better place for you to live in.'

Now Abraham might have said something like, 'Where?' or 'How far?' or 'Thank you very much, but I'm quite happy here.' But he didn't. In fact, he said nothing at all. He just gathered up his wife and his servants and his camels and his sheep, and went where God led him.

Why? Because Abraham trusted God. It was as simple as that.

Canaan was the name of the place where God led Abraham. 'A land flowing with milk and honey' is what some people called it. Which means that there were many cows and goats and bees there, and plenty of flowers and grass for the animals to eat. It was altogether a pretty place. Even nicer than Haran. And Abraham liked it very much.

The only problem was that Abraham had no children. And besides that, both he and his wife, Sarah, were very old. Grandpa- and Grandma-old, and maybe even older than that.

But Abraham trusted God. So one night God said to him, 'Abraham, look up. Do you see the stars? One day you will have so many children and grandchildren and great-grandchildren that counting the stars will be an easy job compared with counting them.

'Now Abraham, look down. Do you see the ground? One day, there will be more members of your family than there are bits of earth on that ground.'

What did Abraham do? He chuckled, that's what. He giggled, he chortled, he laughed! 'Me and my wife have children?' he cackled. 'We're much too old for that!'

But God wasn't joking. 'You will, indeed, have a son,' he said. 'And through your family, I will do something wonderful for the world!'

So Abraham trusted God, and it wasn't long before God sent three messengers to visit him. Abraham was very kind to them. He washed their feet, which was the polite thing to do in those days. Then he served them fresh baked bread and a creamy beef stew. It was delicious! And as the visitors were patting their tummies and wiping their mouths, they said, 'We will be back next year and when we return, Sarah will give birth to a son!'

Someone giggled. Someone chortled. Someone laughed. But it wasn't Abraham this time. It was Sarah, who had been listening in the tent nearby!

And, the next year, when God's promise came true and the baby was born, there was laughter again. So much laughter, in fact, that 'Laughter' is what they decided to call their son. For that is what the name 'Isaac' means.

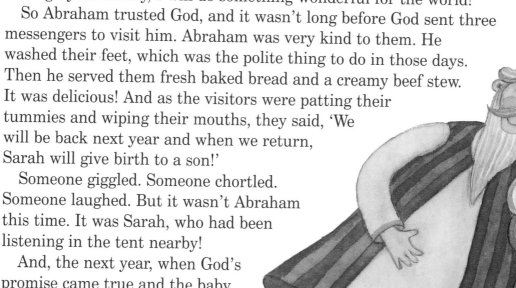

The Bad Brother

Isaac had two sons.

The older son's name was Esau – which means 'Hairy'.

And the younger son's name was Jacob – which means something like 'Cheat'.

Isaac liked Esau the best because he was big and strong (and hairy!) and could hunt.

One day, when Isaac was old and blind, he asked Esau to go and kill an animal, cook the meat and bring it to him.

'When you have done that,' he promised, 'I shall tell you what you will get after I die.'

Esau ran off, his bow slung over his shoulder and his hunting knife in his hand. But he was in such a hurry that he did not notice his mother, Rebecca, hiding behind the tent.

Which son did Rebecca like best? Jacob, of course. Partly because he stayed at home to help her. And partly because he was clever and sneaky, just like her.

Rebecca decided then and there that Isaac's promise to Esau should go to Jacob instead. So she went and found Jacob.

Together they plotted and planned. And in no time at all, Isaac had a visitor with a steaming plate of meat.

'Back so soon, my boy? My, that meat smells delicious. Bring it here at once, Esau.'

The son brought the meat to his father. The son set it down. But the son was not Esau.

'Here you are, Father,' said Jacob in as gruff a voice as he could muster. But the old man was not fooled. Isaac may have been blind, but he was not yet deaf.

'Is that really you, Esau? Come here and let me touch those hairy arms.'

Jacob came closer. He stretched out his arms. And wrapped around them were the hairy skins from an old goat! Isaac touched the arms. He felt the hairy skin. And he smiled.

'It *is* you, Esau!' he said. 'Well then, here is my promise. When I am gone, you will have my land and grow many crops. And besides that, I am putting you in charge of the whole family. They must do whatever you tell them!'

Jacob could hardly believe it! So, when his father had kissed him, he ran off to tell his mother. And it was a good thing, for not a minute later, Esau came to his father with another plate of meat.

'I'm back!' he said cheerfully. 'And I can't wait to hear your promise.'

'What?' exclaimed Isaac. 'I've already given my promise away!' And he told Esau what had happened.

Esau listened and, bit by bit, his face grew as red as his hair. 'Jacob!' he shouted. 'You cheat! One day I will kill you for this!'

But God was watching. And he had something very different in mind.

The Runaway

Jacob ran.

Jacob ran and ran.

Jacob had cheated his brother, Esau. And now his brother wanted to kill him. So Jacob ran.

God watched.

God watched and watched.

God watched Jacob run. And when Jacob was tired and could run no further, when Jacob fell exhausted on the desert floor with only a stone for a pillow, when Jacob was finally ready to listen, God spoke.

He came to Jacob in a dream. There was a ladder, reaching right up to heaven, with angels parading up and down. And at the very top of the ladder stood God himself!

'Jacob,' he said. 'I am the God of your father, Isaac, and your grandfather Abraham. And I am here to make you the same promise I made to them.

'This land is yours. Your family will be great. And one day, through your family, I will do something wonderful for the whole world! Now go and don't be afraid, for you can always count on me to protect you.'

Jacob woke up, amazed. He said 'thank you' to God and he left a stone to mark that special place.

Then Jacob ran.

He ran and ran – all the way to his Uncle Laban's house, where his mother had told him he would be safe. And where God knew he would learn an important lesson.

Now Laban had two daughters.

The older daughter's name was Leah – which means 'Tired'.

The younger daughter's name was Rachel – which means 'Lamb'.

Rachel was beautiful. And the moment Jacob set eyes on her, he knew she was the girl for him!

'Wonderful!' said his Uncle Laban. 'Work for me for seven years, and she will be your wife.'

Seven years passed, but Jacob was so in love with Rachel that it seemed no longer than a day.

The wedding was well attended. The dress was beautiful. But when Jacob pulled aside the veil that hid his bride's face, he found himself looking into Leah's tired eyes!

'Oh, I forgot to mention,' grinned Laban. 'Leah is my eldest daughter, so she has to marry first. But you can marry Rachel, next week if you like, as long as you promise to work for me for another seven years.'

Jacob looked at the ground. Now the cheater knew how it felt to be cheated.

What else could Jacob do? He waited a week, married Rachel, and worked another seven years for his Uncle Laban. Then he headed home, a very different man from the one who had run away.

Jacob walked.

Jacob walked and walked.

And when his home was no more than a day's walk away, he saw Esau, his brother, walking towards him.

Jacob told his family to stay behind, and walked ahead to face his brother's anger. He wasn't running now. He believed that God would protect him.

And so God did – because Esau was different too. When he saw Jacob, he ran up to him, reached out his hairy arms and hugged him!

'I'm sorry,' said Jacob.

'I forgive you,' Esau answered.

And the two sons of Isaac became brothers at last.

21

Joseph the Dreamer

Jacob had twelve sons. That's right – twelve!

His favourite son was Joseph. Jacob spoiled him and gave him special gifts – like a beautiful coat decorated with many colours.

Reds and greens. Blues and yellows. Purples and pinks. Joseph was bright as a rainbow and proud as a peacock.

Joseph's older brothers did not like this one bit. But what they hated even more were Joseph's dreams!

'I had a dream last night,' boasted Joseph.

'Oh no,' groaned his brothers.

'I dreamed that we were all bundles of wheat. And guess what happened? Your bundles of wheat bowed down and worshipped mine!'

'And I had another dream,' Joseph bragged.

'Go on,' his brothers sighed.

'I dreamed we were all stars. And guess what? Your stars bowed down to mine, just as if I were your king!'

It didn't take long for Joseph's brothers to grow tired of this. But that's no excuse for what they did.

The next time they were out of Jacob's sight, they grabbed Joseph, tore off his colourful coat and dropped him down a dry well. They were just about to kill him, in fact, when they spotted a cloud of dust at the edge of the hill. It was a band of traders bound for Egypt, their camels loaded with goods for sale.

'Why should we kill Joseph,' asked one of the brothers, 'when we can sell him to these traders and make some money for ourselves? He'll be sold as a slave in Egypt and his foolish dreams will never come true!'

Twenty pieces of silver. That's how much the traders gave them for Joseph. And when the traders had gone, the brothers ripped up Joseph's coat, dipped it in the blood of a goat and carried it home to their father.

'Joseph is dead,' they told Jacob. And they showed him Joseph's coat, its long sleeves shredded, its beautiful colours smeared with blood.

Jacob wept and wept.

And Joseph wept too, as the traders carried him far from home.

Joseph the Prisoner

When the traders took Joseph to Egypt they sold him to one of the king's own soldiers – a man named Potiphar. He was kind, and Joseph worked very hard for him. So hard, in fact, that Potiphar put Joseph in charge of all his other slaves.

Potiphar's wife, however, was evil and cruel. She told lies about Joseph and had him thrown in prison!

Things looked bad for Joseph. It seemed as if his dreams would never come true. But God was watching over him.

One morning, one of the other prisoners said, 'I had a dream last night. A strange dream. I dreamed I saw a grapevine with three branches. Suddenly, bunches of grapes burst out of those branches. So I squeezed them into a cup and gave it to the king to drink. I wonder what it means?'

Joseph listened to the dream. God listened too. Then he whispered the dream's meaning into Joseph's ear.

'I know what it means!' said Joseph. 'Before you were sent to prison you served wine to the king. Well, in three days, you will be set free and serve him wine once more.'

That's exactly what happened. And when the wine-server was set free, he promised to help Joseph get out too.

Two long years went by. Then, one morning, the king of Egypt said, 'I had a dream last night. A strange dream! And I can't work out what it means.'

'A dream?' said his wine-server. 'I know a man who can tell you all about your dreams.'

And straight away Joseph was brought from the prison.

'I was standing on the banks of the river,' the king told Joseph, 'when I saw

24

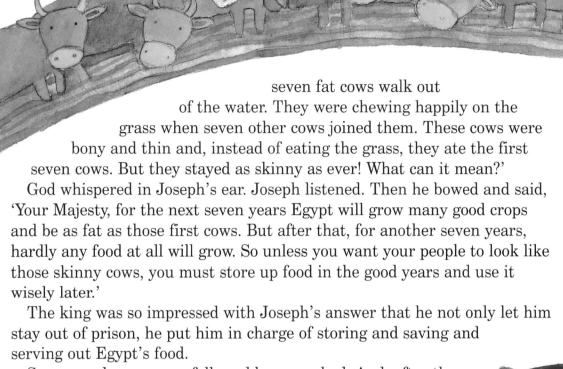

seven fat cows walk out
of the water. They were chewing happily on the
grass when seven other cows joined them. These cows were
bony and thin and, instead of eating the grass, they ate the first
seven cows. But they stayed as skinny as ever! What can it mean?'

God whispered in Joseph's ear. Joseph listened. Then he bowed and said,
'Your Majesty, for the next seven years Egypt will grow many good crops
and be as fat as those first cows. But after that, for another seven years,
hardly any food at all will grow. So unless you want your people to look like
those skinny cows, you must store up food in the good years and use it
wisely later.'

The king was so impressed with Joseph's answer that he not only let him
stay out of prison, he put him in charge of storing and saving and
serving out Egypt's food.

Seven good years *were* followed by seven bad. And, after the
king, Joseph became the most important man in Egypt. It was
like a dream come true!

Joseph the Ruler

One day there was a knock at Joseph's door. And when he answered it, his eleven brothers were standing there!

They bowed down before him. They kissed his feet. And they begged, 'Kind sir, we have come to Egypt all the way from the land of Canaan. We have no food. We are starving. May we please buy some from you?'

Joseph said nothing. He just stared at his brothers. He knew who they were, but they did not recognize him.

'All right,' said Joseph, in his sternest voice. 'I will sell you food.' And he ordered his servants to load his brothers' animals.

But that wasn't all he told them to do. 'Take one of my silver cups,' he said, 'and hide it in the sack of food tied to the youngest lad's donkey.' Joseph had a plan. He wanted to see if his brothers had changed.

When Joseph's brothers reached the edge of the city, his servants stopped them and searched through their sacks. What did they find? The silver cup, of course!

'We don't know how it got there!' the brothers exclaimed to Joseph.

'Your brother stole it, that's how,' Joseph answered. 'So he must stay here in Egypt and be my slave.'

'No, please,' begged the brothers. 'That would break our father's heart. Keep one of us instead.'

When Joseph heard that, he knew his brothers had changed. So he told them who he was, right then and there.

'I am Joseph,' he announced, 'your long-lost brother.'

This news did not make his brothers feel any better. They were so frightened, in fact, that they could hardly speak.

'Don't be afraid,' said Joseph, 'I forgive you. You meant to hurt me, but God used what you did to save us all from this terrible famine. Now, go. Fetch my father and the rest of our family to come and live in Egypt with me.'

The brothers looked up.

The brothers grinned.

The brothers cheered!

And after a lot of hugging and hello-ing and handshaking, they set off for Canaan to tell Jacob the good news.

And Joseph? Joseph just sat back on his throne and smiled. And thanked God for making his dreams come true.

The Secret Baby

There was a basket in the water.
  There was a baby in the basket!
  The baby's big sister was watching from the river bank.
  And God was watching too.

Why was the basket in the water?
  Why was the baby in the basket?
  Because the baby was a Hebrew – a great, great, great grandson of Abraham, Isaac and Jacob.
  'There are too many Israelites in Egypt,' the king said to his soldiers.
'If we are not careful, there will soon be more of them than of us!
So I want you to kill every baby Hebrew boy.'
  Some Hebrew mothers cried.
  Some Hebrew mothers ran.
  But this baby's mother was clever.
  She covered a basket with tar – so it would not sink.
  She laid her baby in the basket – and prayed that he would be quiet.
      And she hid the basket in the reeds near the river bank
          and hoped no one would notice.

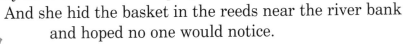

            But someone did.
          And not just *any* someone. The
        daughter of the king himself!
            She went to the river to bathe.
            She spotted the basket boat.
            She sent her servant to fetch it out.
            And when she looked into it – oh, what
        a surprise!

The baby's big sister hid her eyes. She could not bear to watch.

But God kept watching. He had special plans for this baby.

'I don't care if this baby is a Hebrew,' the king's daughter announced. 'I want to keep him. Coochie-coochie-coo. I shall call him Moses. But I will need a serving woman to feed him and look after him…'

And that's when God nudged the baby's big sister, just enough so she'd jump up from where she'd been hiding.

'A serving woman?' she shouted, almost before she thought. 'I know a serving woman who can help you.'

'Well then, fetch her, girl,' commanded the princess.

And God just smiled. For now little Moses would be raised by his own mother, taught the Hebrew ways, and be ready for that day when God would use him to set his people free.

The Burning Bush

The sun was burning hot.

Moses' skin was burned dark brown.

And suddenly, he saw it – a bright red burning bush!

Its branches crackled orange and red, and Moses could not help but watch – for the bush did not burn up!

'Take off your shoes,' came a voice from the bush. 'This is a very special place.'

'Who are you?' asked Moses. 'And why are you talking to me? I am just a poor shepherd.'

'I am the God of Abraham, Isaac and Jacob – the God of Israel,' the voice replied. 'And you are more than a shepherd. You are Moses, the man I have chosen to lead my people out of Egypt.'

'I can't do that,' Moses trembled. 'I left Egypt years ago, and I'm an old man now.'

'You can do it. You must do it,' God answered, 'for my people are slaves in Egypt and have prayed to be set free. I have heard their prayers, and you are the man I have chosen.'

'But what if I go and they don't believe you sent me?' Moses asked.

'Take the walking stick that's in your hand,' God said, 'and throw it on the ground.'

Moses did as God told him – and the stick turned into a wriggling snake!

'Now pick it up,' God commanded.

Moses wrapped a shaking hand around the snake's scaly middle – and it turned back into a stick!

'Show them that!' God laughed. 'Then they'll believe you.'

'But I'm so shy,' Moses continued. 'I'm no good at talking to people.'

'Don't worry about that,' God assured him. 'Your brother Aaron loves to talk. You can take him with you. Now, go! My people need your help.'

So Moses went. He put on his shoes. He picked up his walking stick. And he went – off to set God's people free.

The Great Escape

Moses and Aaron went to visit the king of Egypt.

'God wants you to set his people free,' they announced.

But the king just laughed. 'Don't be silly,' he said. 'They do what I tell them. They work for nothing. I will never set them free.'

'Then I must warn you,' said Moses, 'God will make some very bad things happen until you change your mind.'

It started almost at once. The rivers of Egypt filled with blood. The houses of Egypt swarmed with frogs. The dust of Egypt turned into gnats.

But the king would not let God's people go.

The people in Egypt were covered with flies. The animals in Egypt grew sick and died. And ugly sores broke out on everyone.

But still the king would not let God's people go.

Hail pelted the land and broke down the crops. Locusts gobbled up what was left. Then darkness like night fell for three whole days.

And still the king would not give in.

Finally, God sent an angel to kill the king's eldest son. And the eldest sons of the rest of the Egyptians.

Then, at last, the king said, 'Go! Go, and never come back!'

God's people cheered. God's people packed. God's people waved goodbye. But just as they reached the sea and were puzzling out how to get across, the king changed his mind!

He leaped into his chariot and led his army out after them. Soon, the sea stretched out before God's people and the Egyptian army rushed behind them like a wave. What could they do?

'Raise your special walking stick,' God whispered to Moses. And as Moses did so, the sea split in two before them – leaving a path right down the middle! The Hebrews hurried along that path to the other side, the Egyptian army close behind. Just as the last of God's people had safely crossed, Moses lowered his stick, the waters rushed back, and the army was washed away.

God's people were free at last!

A Long Journey

'We're hot,' the people complained.

'We're hungry,' they moaned.

'Where are we going, anyway?' they wondered.

Moses just sighed and shook his head.

God had set the Hebrews free. And now he was leading them through the wilderness back to their own special land – the land he had given to Abraham, Isaac and Jacob.

They should have been grateful. They should have been glad.

But all they could do was moan.

'We're tired.'

'We're thirsty.'

'Are we there yet?'

So Moses prayed to God. And God answered.

He made fresh water spill out of dry rocks!

He sent plump meaty quail at dinner time.

And, for breakfast, he covered the ground with sweet white flakes. (The people called this 'manna' – a word that means, 'This tastes good – whatever it is!')

Did the Hebrews stop complaining? Not for one minute.

'We're lost.'

'We're scared.'

'We should have stayed in Egypt.'

'Don't be ridiculous!' said Moses. 'God has promised to take us to our own special land. And he has chosen us to be his own special people. We can trust him to do the very best for us.'

And so God did.

By day, he led them with a thick white cloud. By night, a flaming torch. And he showed his people the way through the wilderness.

Then God called Moses to the top of a mountain, and gave him ten important rules that showed his people how to live a good and happy life.

And finally, God showed them plans for a tabernacle – a special tent where they could worship him and praise his name.

This should have helped. It really should have. But God's people just kept on moaning.

'What's going to happen?'

'Why is it taking so long?'

And even, 'Maybe we should follow a different God.'

In fact, God's people moaned the whole journey long – right up to the moment they reached the border of God's Promised Land.

Spies in Canaan

When the Hebrews finally arrived at the edge of the land their God had promised them, they were still not happy.

'We're worried.'

'We're frightened.'

'What if something bad happens when we get there?'

So they asked Moses to send spies into the land. They wanted to know exactly what lay ahead.

There were twelve spies, one for each of the Hebrew tribes.

They tiptoed into the Promised Land. They hid behind bushes. They peeped out from behind boulders. And they had a good look around. Then they sneaked back across the border and told their people about everything that they had seen.

At first, their reports sounded good.

'The land is wonderful!'

'There's loads of food!'

'Just look at the size of these grapes!'

But some of the spies had other things to say.

'The cities are surrounded by enormous walls!'

'The people are giants!'

'And they make us look like tiny little grasshoppers!'

'Wait!' cried two other spies, whose names were Joshua and Caleb. 'God has promised this land to us and he will help us to win it, no matter how big our enemies are.'

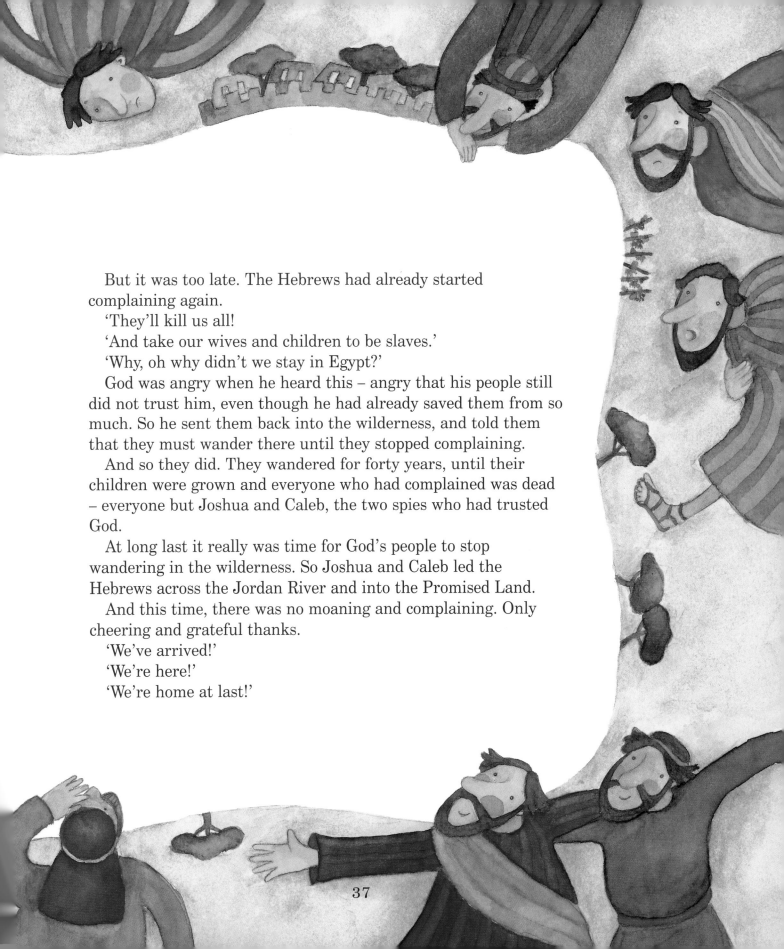

But it was too late. The Hebrews had already started complaining again.

'They'll kill us all!

'And take our wives and children to be slaves.'

'Why, oh why didn't we stay in Egypt?'

God was angry when he heard this – angry that his people still did not trust him, even though he had already saved them from so much. So he sent them back into the wilderness, and told them that they must wander there until they stopped complaining.

And so they did. They wandered for forty years, until their children were grown and everyone who had complained was dead – everyone but Joshua and Caleb, the two spies who had trusted God.

At long last it really was time for God's people to stop wandering in the wilderness. So Joshua and Caleb led the Hebrews across the Jordan River and into the Promised Land.

And this time, there was no moaning and complaining. Only cheering and grateful thanks.

'We've arrived!'

'We're here!'

'We're home at last!'

The Walls Fall Down

The walls of Jericho went round and round. Round and round the whole city. The walls were tall. The walls were thick. How would God's people ever get in?

Joshua's thoughts went round and round. Round and round inside his head. He was the leader of God's people now that Moses was dead. But how could he lead them into Jericho?

The sword of the Lord swung round and round. Round and round the angel's head. 'God will lead you into Jericho,' said the angel to Joshua. 'He has a secret plan. All you have to do is trust him.'

The soldiers of Israel gathered round and round. Round and round their leader, Joshua. He told them the angel's plan. He didn't leave out one bit. The soldiers were amazed!

So the army of Israel marched round and round. Round and round the walls of Jericho. Once round each day. Six days in a row. And the people of Jericho laughed.

'Why are they marching round and round? Round and round the walls of Jericho? Is this a parade? Is it some kind of trick? They'll never beat us this way!'

But when the army marched round and round, round and round on the seventh day – they marched round once, they marched round twice. They marched round Jericho seven times. Then they raised their voices. They blew their trumpets. And the walls came crashing down!

The people of Israel danced round and round. Round and round the ruins of Jericho. 'God is our helper!' they sang and they shouted. 'He will never let us down!'

39

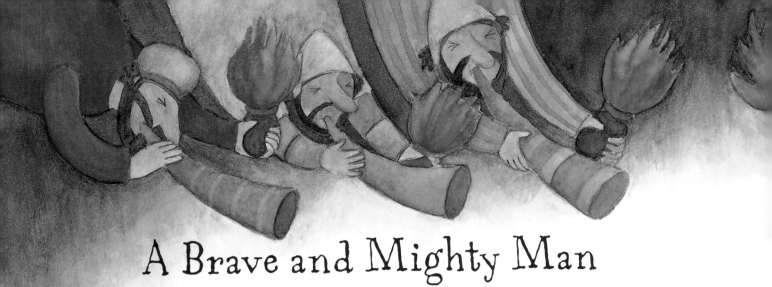

A Brave and Mighty Man

'Gideon,' God whispered. 'Oh, Gideon,' God called. 'I need your help, you brave and mighty man.'

But Gideon was nowhere to be found. As a matter of fact, he was hiding – in a pit his father used for crushing grapes.

'You can't be talking to me,' Gideon stammered. 'I'm no brave and mighty man.'

But God knew what he was doing. He always does.

'You're the man all right,' God said. 'The Midianites have my people surrounded and I want you to round up an army to stop them!'

Gideon did what God told him. And, to his surprise, over thirty thousand men agreed to join him!

'Gideon,' God whispered. 'Oh, Gideon,' God called. 'You have far too many men. I want you to send some of them away.'

'There are more Midianites than I can count!' Gideon stammered. 'I need all the help I can get.'

But God knew what he was doing. He always does.

'I am all the help you need,' God said. 'So tell the men who are frightened to go home.'

Gideon did what God told him. And when he had finished, there were only ten thousand left.

'Gideon,' God whispered. 'Oh, Gideon,' God called. 'You still have too many men. So here's what I want you to do…'

Gideon listened to God's plan. Gideon stammered and shook. Then he led his men to the

river and told them to have a drink.

Some soldiers lapped up the water like dogs; Gideon sent them home.

Others got down on their knees and scooped up the water in their hands. Those were the soldiers Gideon kept. And when he had finished, there were only three hundred left!

'Gideon,' God whispered. 'Oh, Gideon,' God called. 'Now we are ready to fight the Midianites.'

'But there are thousands of them,' Gideon stammered. 'And only three hundred of us. How can we possibly win?'

'You can't,' God said. 'Not without my help. And that's what I want you to see. Now, listen. Here's my plan…'

Later that night, Gideon led his three hundred men to the edge of the Midianite camp. In one hand every soldier carried a trumpet and in the other hand an earthenware pot with a flaming torch inside. There wasn't a sword in sight! At Gideon's signal, the soldiers blew their trumpets, smashed their pots and shouted, 'For the Lord and for Gideon!'

The Midianite soldiers awoke, startled.

It seemed as if there was noise and fire all around them! Dazed and confused, they stumbled about in the dark – into each other and over each other. And it wasn't long before they were fighting each other too!

When all the fighting had stopped, the Midianite soldiers who were left ran away, convinced that they had been defeated by some great army. But it was only Gideon, his three hundred men and a God who knew what he was doing all along.

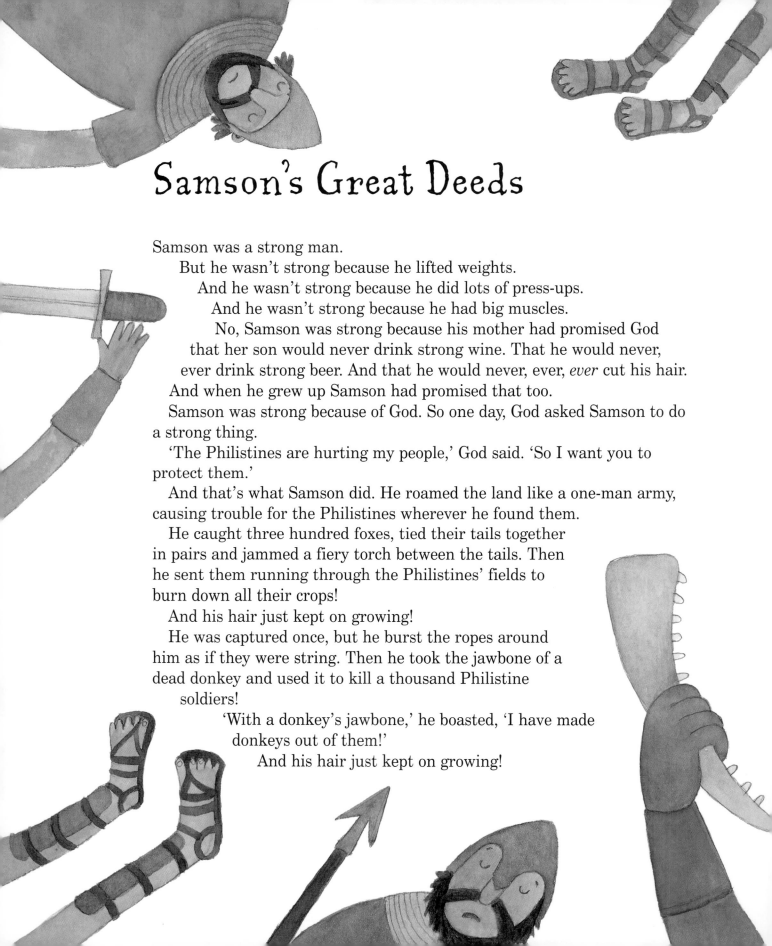

Samson's Great Deeds

Samson was a strong man.

But he wasn't strong because he lifted weights.

And he wasn't strong because he did lots of press-ups.

And he wasn't strong because he had big muscles.

No, Samson was strong because his mother had promised God that her son would never drink strong wine. That he would never, ever drink strong beer. And that he would never, ever, *ever* cut his hair. And when he grew up Samson had promised that too.

Samson was strong because of God. So one day, God asked Samson to do a strong thing.

'The Philistines are hurting my people,' God said. 'So I want you to protect them.'

And that's what Samson did. He roamed the land like a one-man army, causing trouble for the Philistines wherever he found them.

He caught three hundred foxes, tied their tails together in pairs and jammed a fiery torch between the tails. Then he sent them running through the Philistines' fields to burn down all their crops!

And his hair just kept on growing!

He was captured once, but he burst the ropes around him as if they were string. Then he took the jawbone of a dead donkey and used it to kill a thousand Philistine soldiers!

'With a donkey's jawbone,' he boasted, 'I have made donkeys out of them!'

And his hair just kept on growing!

And when the Philistines thought they had him surrounded in the city of Gaza, he tore the enormous doors off the city gates and escaped, carrying them to the top of a hill!

And his hair just kept on growing!

For twenty years, Samson protected God's people – protected them with his mighty deeds. Protected them with the strength God gave him.

And his hair just kept on growing!

43

Samson and Delilah

The Philistines were tired of Samson beating them all the time, so they went to talk to Samson's girlfriend, Delilah.

'If you can find the secret to his strength,' they said, 'we will give you a great big pile of silver!'

Delilah liked silver. She liked it even better than she liked Samson. So she did what they asked.

'Samson. Oh Samson,' Delilah cooed. 'Please tell me the secret of your strength.'

Now Samson liked Delilah a lot. But he wasn't stupid. So he decided to play a little trick on her.

'Tie me up with seven fresh bow strings,' he lied, 'and I will be as weak as any man.'

So Delilah hid some men in the next room. She tied up Samson with seven fresh bow strings. Then she cried, 'Samson! Oh Samson! The Philistines are coming!'

The Philistines burst through the door! Samson burst the bow strings! Then he chased them all away.

And his hair just kept on growing!

'Samson. Oh Samson,' Delilah pouted. 'You lied to me. Tell me, please, the true secret of your strength.'

Samson liked this game, so he told her another lie.

'Tie me up with new ropes – and I will be as weak as any man.'

So once again, Delilah hid some men in the next room. She tied up Samson with new ropes. And then she cried, 'Samson! Oh Samson! The Philistines are coming!'

The Philistines burst through the door. Samson burst the ropes as if they were threads. Then he chased them all away.

And his hair just kept on growing!

'Samson. Oh Samson,' Delilah whined. 'You lied to me again! Please, please tell me the secret of your strength.'

Samson grinned. 'All right then,' he said. But it was just another lie. 'Take the seven braids of my hair and weave them into the cloth on your loom. And I will be as weak as any man.'

So Delilah hid more men in the next room. She wove

Samson's seven long braids into the cloth on her loom. And then she cried, 'Samson! Oh Samson! The Philistines are coming!'

The Philistines burst through the door. Samson burst to his feet, loom, cloth and all. Then he chased them all away.

And his hair just kept on growing!

'Samson. Oh Samson,' wept Delilah. 'You don't love me at all! You've lied to me again. Please, please, please tell me the secret of your strength.' And she nagged him day after day after day.

Maybe it was the nagging. Maybe it was the tears. Maybe Samson truly loved Delilah. Or maybe Samson just forgot where his strength really came from. Maybe he thought it was all down to him – and not the God he'd made his promise to. Whatever the reason, Samson finally told Delilah the truth.

'I made a promise once,' he said. 'That a razor would never touch my head. If you cut my hair I will be as weak as any man.'

So once again Delilah hid some men in the next room. And when Samson fell asleep, she told one of the men to cut off his seven long braids.

'Samson! Oh Samson!' she cried. 'The Philistines are coming!'

Samson woke. 'I'll chase them away, just like before!' he boasted. But when the Philistines burst through the door, Samson could do nothing. He really was as weak as any man.

And this time the Philistines carried him off to prison.

Samson and the Philistines

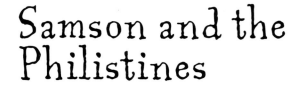

When the Philistines captured Samson, they poked out his eyes, bound him with strong ropes and threw him in a prison cell. They chained him to a great stone wheel, and day after day, he pushed the wheel to grind their corn. They thought they had beaten him for good. But Samson's hair began to grow again. And week by week, month by month, his hair just kept on growing!

Some time later, the Philistines decided to have a big party to celebrate Samson's capture and to thank their god Dagon for delivering him into their hands. What they didn't count on was the one true God. The God who had given Samson his strength and who still wanted to use him to protect his people.

There were more than three thousand Philistines gathered in the temple on that day. The place was packed. And in the middle of the celebration, the rulers had Samson dragged before them. The people laughed and clapped when they saw him.

'Our god has beaten our enemy,' they cheered. 'The one who caused us so much trouble.'

And when they were done laughing, Samson was dragged to stand near the pillars of the temple. But Samson had one more idea – one last clever plan to defeat his enemies.

'You know I'm blind,' said Samson to the man who guarded him. 'Put me where I can feel the pillars, please, so I can lean against them.'

So that's what the servant did. He stood Samson between the pillars – the pillars that supported the whole of the temple.

'Dear Lord,' prayed Samson. 'The only strength I ever had came from you. I remember that now. So I ask that you remember me and give me that strength just one more time.'

And with his left hand on one pillar and his right hand on another, he began to push.

He pushed, and the pillars creaked.

He pushed, and the pillars cracked.

He pushed, and the pillars crumbled.

He pushed, and the pillars collapsed.

And when they did, the whole of the temple came crashing down with them! It crashed down on the Philistines. It crashed down on their rulers. And, sadly, it crashed down on Samson too.

'Let me die with the Philistines!' Samson cried to heaven. And so he did, killing many more with his death than he had ever done in his life, and doing what God had asked him to – protecting his people from their enemy.

Ruth Finds a New Home

Naomi was lonely. Her husband was dead. So were her two sons. And she was living in a country that was far from home with her sons' widows, Orpah and Ruth.

'I'm going home,' said Naomi to her daughters-in-law one day. 'Back to my own country. Back to Bethlehem, where I belong. You must stay here. I will miss you, but this is your country, not mine.'

Naomi expected Orpah and Ruth to kiss her and hug her and wave goodbye. And that is just what Orpah did. But Ruth did something different.

She kissed Naomi, and she hugged Naomi, and then she said, 'I'm coming with you.'

'Why?' asked Naomi. 'Why leave your people and your home to travel to a place you do not know? Here you have a chance of finding another husband. But I can't give you one.'

But no matter what Naomi said, Ruth would not change her mind. She cared for Naomi and wanted to make sure that she returned home safe and sound.

'I'm going with you,' she said. 'And that's all there is to it. From now on, your people will be my people and your God will be my God.'

So Naomi and Ruth went to Bethlehem. And while Naomi greeted her relatives, Ruth went off to find a job. But that was hard because she came from a different country. So she ended up gathering bits of barley in a field that belonged to a man named Boaz – bits

that were left behind when the workers collected the grain.

Boaz soon noticed Ruth. He had heard about what she'd done for Naomi. He admired her courage and her loyalty. And he also took a shine to her. And that is why the next day he told his workers that they should leave a bit more barley behind, on purpose. Now Ruth would have more to take home with her.

Ruth was delighted. And when she told Naomi what had happened, and when she showed Naomi all the barley she'd found, Naomi asked her who the field belonged to.

'A man named Boaz,' said Ruth.

And now Naomi was delighted too. Because Boaz was one of her relatives! And in a flash, Naomi turned from mother-in-law to matchmaker.

'Put on your best dress,' she told Ruth. 'And a little perfume too. You're going to visit Boaz tonight!'

And so Ruth did. And Boaz liked her so much that he immediately arranged to marry her.

Ruth was delighted. And Naomi was too. For God had rewarded Ruth's loyalty, and had given her both a husband and a home.

And what is more, Ruth gave birth to a son whose name was Obed. And Obed's son was Jesse. And one of Jesse's sons was a shepherd boy named David, who ran into a giant one day. But that's another story!

Samuel Hears a Voice

Now that God's people were living in their own land, there were so many things he wanted to tell them:

How to be happy.

How to take care of each other.

How to protect themselves from their enemies.

So God decided to choose someone to speak for him.

Someone he could talk to, who would then go and talk to the people. Someone called a prophet.

God looked and looked all over the land of Israel, eager to pick just the right person. And finally, he found him.

In the village of Shiloh.

In the house of Eli, the priest.

A little boy!

'Samuel,' God called, one night. 'Samuel, I want to talk with you.'

Samuel sat up and rubbed his sleepy eyes. He'd never heard God's voice before and he thought that old Eli was calling him.

Samuel stumbled into Eli's room to see what he wanted. But Eli just shooed him back to bed.

'Samuel,' God called again, 'Samuel, listen.'

Samuel was confused this time. And a little scared. So he crept back into Eli's room.

'I told you, boy,' yawned the old priest. 'I didn't call you. Now off to bed!'

Samuel didn't know what to think as he crawled under his covers. But when God called, 'Samuel, Samuel,' for the third time, he knew what to do.

He dashed back to Eli, just as fast as he could!

'Samuel,' sighed Eli, 'if either of us is going to get any sleep tonight, we need to find out who's calling you. And I have an idea who it might be. So the next time you hear that voice, I don't want you to come running in here. Instead, I want you to say, "Speak, Lord, and I will listen." '

Samuel's eyes opened wide.

'You mean it's God who's calling me?'

'Do as I tell you,' said Eli, 'and we'll find out.'

So Samuel went back to bed.

God called his name again.

This time Samuel stayed there and listened to God, and his eyes opened wide with wonder.

And from that moment until Samuel was himself an old man, God talked to Samuel, giving him messages to pass on to the people. And, just like the first time, God's messages never failed to leave him wide-eyed with wonder.

Samuel the Kingmaker

With God's help, Samuel led God's people. But when Samuel grew old, the people asked him for something that made him sad.

'Everybody else has a king,' they said. 'So why can't we have a king too?'

Samuel told God about this, and God helped him to feel better.

'It's not you they don't want,' God said. 'It's me. I'm their true king, but sometimes they just can't see it. So tell the people they can have a king if they want. But tell them the truth. Tell them that it won't make their lives any easier.'

So that's what Samuel did.

'God says you can have a king,' he told the people. 'But he wants you to know what that will mean.

'A king will turn your sons into soldiers, your daughters into housemaids, and your grain and your gold into gifts for his special friends. In other words, he will make you his slaves.'

It didn't sound very nice, but the people still wanted a king. So Samuel found them one – a tall and handsome man named Saul.

Saul did well for a while. But then he stopped listening to Samuel and he stopped obeying God. So God told Samuel to find another king.

'Go to Bethlehem,' God said. 'Find a man named Jesse. If the people must have a king, then it should be someone who loves me, and trusts me, and will follow me. That someone is one of Jesse's sons.'

So Samuel went to Bethlehem. And when he laid his eyes on Jesse's oldest son, Eliab, Samuel was sure that Eliab was the one.

God was sure too – sure that Samuel was wrong!

'He may be tall,' God said. 'But so was Saul. And remember how he turned out.'

And then God said something very important.

'You can only see what people look like on the outside, Samuel. But I can look inside them – deep down into their hearts. And it's what is on the inside of a person that matters most to me.'

So Samuel moved on to Jesse's other sons, while God looked into their hearts.

'How about the second son?' said Samuel.

'No,' said God. 'Try again'

'The third son?'

'Afraid not.'

'The fourth son?'

'No way!'

'The fifth son?'

'You must be joking!'

'The sixth son?'

'Not a chance.'

'The seventh son?' asked Samuel. 'He's the only one left!'

'You'll have to look harder,' said God. 'Because he's not the one, either.'

'I don't suppose you have any more sons?' Samuel asked.

'Well, there's the youngest,' Jesse answered. 'But he's out in the field, looking after the sheep.'

'Fetch him!' said Samuel. 'Quick as you can!'

And when the boy appeared, God whispered to Samuel, 'That's the one! His heart is pure and true and he longs to follow me.'

So Samuel poured oil on the head of Jesse's youngest son – as a sign that God wanted him to do something special and that one day he would be king.

And the youngest son's name was David.

David the Giant-Killer

Goliath was big.

He had to stoop to get through doorways. His head was always bumping up against the ceiling. And his friends thought twice before inviting him to dinner.

Goliath had a big spear. Ten feet long, at least. With a big iron point. And his big bronze armour weighed a hundred pounds or more.

Goliath had a big voice, too.

And, one day, he used it. He stamped out in front of his army of Philistines and shouted across the valley to the soldiers camped on the other side.

'I am Goliath!' he bellowed. 'And I dare any of you to come and fight me. Win the fight, and we will be your slaves. Lose, and you must work for us.'

David was little.

Just a boy, really, who looked after the sheep. When he wanted a break from that, he carried cheese to his brothers in the army. And that's what he was doing one day, when he heard Goliath shout.

David was a little angry.

'Who does that giant think he is?' huffed David. 'Doesn't he know that the Lord God himself watches over us? Why, with God's help, even I could beat that bully.'

So David took a little walk. He went to see the king.

'I want to fight the giant,' he announced.

The king almost fell off his throne.

'But you are so little,' said the king. 'And he is so big!'

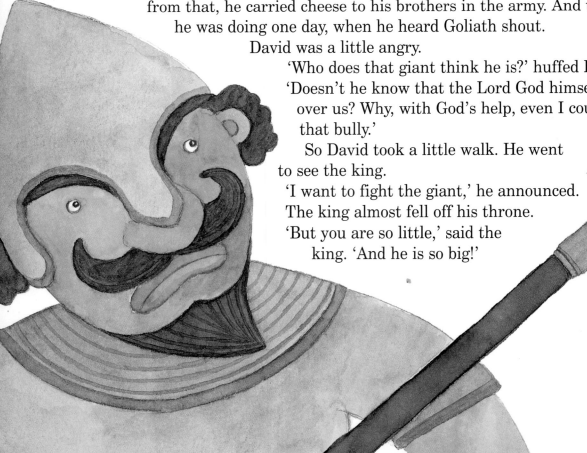

'A lion is big,' answered David. 'And so is a bear. But when they came after my sheep, the Lord God helped me face them and fight them off. He will do the same with this giant.'

'All right,' the king agreed. 'But at least let me lend you my armour.'

The armour was big. Too big. And so heavy that David could hardly move.

So he gave it back. And picked up five little stones instead. And a sling. And his trusty shepherd's staff.

Goliath gave a big laugh when he saw the little shepherd boy.

And he took two big steps.

David ran a little way.

Two more giant steps for Goliath.

And David ran a little further.

They were in the middle of the valley now, and everything was quiet.

Goliath roared a big roar, sucked in a big breath of air, and raised his big spear.

David sneaked his little hand into his little pouch, pulled out a little stone and slipped it in his sling. Then he spun it round his head and let it fly.

And before the giant could say another word, the stone struck him on the head, and he fell with a big thud to the ground.

David's side shouted a big 'Hooray!'

Goliath's side whispered a little 'Uh-oh.'

And from then on, some pretty big things happened to the little shepherd boy. He was given a king's reward. He was promised the hand of the king's daughter in marriage. And, one day, he became king himself! The very best king God's people ever had.

The Wise King

When David died, his son Solomon became Israel's new king. And what do you think was the very first thing he did?

Pass some new law? No.

Send his army to fight some new enemy? Not likely.

Order himself a fancy new crown? Never.

No, the first thing he did was to kneel down before God and pray.

'Good for you!' God said to Solomon. 'Now what would you like me to give you?'

Solomon could have prayed for anything. Anything at all! But what do you think he asked for?

A long life? No.

Victory in battle? Not likely.

Loads of money? Never.

No, the only thing he asked for was... wisdom!

'It's going to be hard ruling over all these people,' he prayed. 'And I want to do the best job that I can. So help me, God. Give me wisdom to make the right choices and do the right things.'

Well, God was so pleased with Solomon's choice that he promised to give him wisdom – *and* all the other things, as well. A long life, victory and loads of money!

It wasn't long before Solomon's wisdom was put to the test.

Two women came to see him one day. One of them was holding a baby. And the other one was very unhappy.

'That woman stole my baby!' she cried. 'Her baby died. So while I was sleeping, she came and took mine!'

'That's a lie!' shouted the woman with the baby. And she held the child even more tightly.

Solomon looked at the women. Solomon looked at the baby. And what do you think he did?

Give the baby to the first woman? No.

Give the baby to the second woman? Not likely.

Keep it for himself? Never.

No, he called one of his soldiers and told him to raise his sword above the child.

'Now cut the baby in half,' Solomon ordered, 'and each of the women can have a piece.'

The soldier was shocked. He looked at the king. He looked at the baby. But before he could use his sword, the woman who claimed her child had been stolen cried, 'Stop! Let her have the child. He's my baby, but I'd rather see him raised by another than have him cut in two.'

'Oh no,' said the woman holding the baby. 'The king is right. Cut the baby in half!'

It was exactly what Solomon had hoped for.

'Now I see who the real mother is,' he said. 'She would rather give up her child than see it harmed.' And he took the baby from one woman and gave it to the other.

And what do you think God's people did?

They clapped.

They cheered.

And they thanked God for giving them a king who was both wise and good.

Elijah and the Ravens

If David was the best king God's people ever had, then Ahab was one of the worst!

He didn't listen to God at all.

No, he worshipped a statue called Baal. And what is worse, he made a lot of God's people do the same.

God was not happy that his people had replaced him with a god who was nothing more than a pile of sticks and stones. So he whispered into the ear of a prophet called Elijah – a man who had not forgotten him.

'Tell King Ahab that what he is doing is wrong. Tell him that I will stop the rain from falling until he stops worshipping Baal.'

Elijah passed God's message on to Ahab. But Ahab just laughed. That is, until it stopped raining!

Now King Ahab was angry with Elijah. So angry that he wanted to kill him. So God told Elijah to hide in a deep ravine, east of the Jordan River.

'But how will I live?' asked Elijah. 'Out in the wilderness and all on my own?'

'I've sorted that,' God answered. 'I'm the real God, after all – remember? Not some statue made of sticks and stones. There's a brook that runs down the middle of the ravine. You can drink from that. And I've asked a few of my feathery friends to feed you.'

Elijah wasn't sure what God meant. But he trusted God to take care of him.

So Elijah crossed the Jordan
and hid in the ravine. He drank from
the brook, just like God had told him to.

And on the very first morning, some of God's
feathery friends came cawing. They were ravens, and in their beaks and
their claws they carried meat and bread for his breakfast.

Elijah ate until he was full. And when evening came, the ravens came
cawing again, with more bread and meat for his tea!

And so Elijah hid safely and never went hungry. God fed Elijah in his
Raven Ravine Restaurant because he was, after all, the real
God, and not some statue made of sticks and stones.

A Jar and a Jug

Elijah survived for a long time in his Raven Ravine Restaurant. But because there was no rain, the brook eventually dried up.

'What now?' Elijah cried to God. 'I'll die of thirst if I stay here!'

'I am the real God – remember?' God said. 'Not some statue made of sticks and stones. So I've planned ahead. There's a widow who lives in Zarephath, not far from here. Go and stay with her. She'll take care of you.'

So Elijah went to Zarephath, and there he found a widow picking sticks up from the ground.

'Excuse me,' he said to her. 'May I have some bread and water, please?'

The woman stopped picking up the sticks and stared at Elijah.

'I don't have any bread,' she said wearily. 'All I have is a handful of flour in a jar and a few drops of oil in a jug. I'm picking up these sticks to make a little fire. I shall mix the flour and the oil into a cake and bake it on the fire. Then my son and I will eat the cake and die. For that is all we have left.'

It was a sad story, and Elijah felt sorry for the widow. But then he remembered. God was the real God. Not some statue made of sticks and stones. And God had told him that the widow would take care of him.

So Elijah told the woman what to do.

'You must trust me,' he said. 'For I serve the real God and he has promised to take care of us. Make me a cake out of what you have in your jar and your jug. Make a cake for yourself and for your son too. And I promise you that what is in the jar and in the jug will never run out!'

The woman trusted Elijah. She did what he told her. And just as he promised, no matter how much flour she took from the jar or how much oil she poured from the jug, there was always some flour and oil left!

And so Elijah lived through the drought, even though it lasted for three whole years – with the help of ravens in a ravine, with oil and flour from a widow's jar and a jug and, most of all, because he trusted the real God and not some statue made of sticks and stones.

God Sends Fire

In the third year of the drought, Elijah went to see King Ahab again.

'Elijah, you troublemaker!' Ahab roared. 'See what you have done! The crops have died. The wells are dry. And it's all your fault!'

'No, Your Majesty,' said Elijah. 'The fault is yours, for you have not obeyed the Lord God.'

'The Lord God – ha!' snapped Ahab. 'I don't have to listen to what he says. I follow Baal.'

'All right, then,' answered Elijah. 'Why don't we have a contest – to prove once and for all who the true God really is?'

And so they did – on the top of Mount Carmel, overlooking the sea. Elijah, prophet of the Lord God, stood on one side. Four hundred and fifty prophets of Baal stood on the other. And the people of Israel gathered around the bottom to watch.

The prophets of Baal went first. They stacked up a pile of wood. They killed a bull and laid it on the top. Then they prayed to Baal, and asked him to set the whole thing on fire. They prayed hard. They prayed long – from breakfast to lunchtime. But there was no fire. Not even a spark.

Elijah couldn't resist having a little fun. 'Perhaps Baal is asleep,' he joked. 'Or day-dreaming, or on holiday! Or maybe he's just a little hard of hearing.'

And so Baal's prophets prayed louder. But it made no difference, and by the middle of the afternoon they were exhausted.

And that's when Elijah took his turn. He piled up twelve stones – one for each of the sons of Jacob. He laid wood on top of that, then the bull. Finally he poured water over the whole thing!

The crowd was amazed. How would it ever catch fire?

But Elijah knew just what he was doing. 'Lord,' he prayed, 'you are the real God and not some statue made of sticks and stones. Please show that to your people now, so they will follow you again.'

Elijah had barely opened his eyes when it happened. God sent fire from heaven that burned up not only the bull, but the water, stones and wood as well!

'The Lord is God!' the people shouted.

Then they cheered for Elijah, chased away the prophets of Baal and ran for cover. Because suddenly it had started to rain!

The Helpful Servant

Naaman was a soldier. Not just any soldier, but the commander of the whole Syrian army! He was a very powerful man. But he was afraid.

Naaman, you see, was ill, and no one knew how to make him well. His skin was covered with sores, and he couldn't feel his fingers or his feet. Everyone felt sorry for him. And God felt sorry, too.

So God whispered to a little girl who had been captured by Naaman's army and carried away from God's Promised Land. She worked for Naaman's wife, and one day she said to her mistress, 'Back in Israel, where I come from, there lives a man called Elisha. God uses him to make sick people well. If only Naaman could go and see him.'

And before long the great soldier, who had fought against God's people, was off to seek help from God's prophet.

Naaman didn't go alone. He took his servants. And his horses. And a chariot full of treasure – to reward Elisha in case his cure should work.

It was a grand parade, and Naaman expected a grand greeting in return. But when he sent one of his men to knock on Elisha's door, the prophet did not even answer. Instead he told his servant Gehazi to say: 'If you want to be well, go and dip yourself seven times in the Jordan River.'

Now it may be that Naaman was tired and frustrated. Or it may be simply that he was proud. Whatever the reason, the prophet's message made him angry.

'The Jordan River?' he shouted. 'It's filthy! I'll throw myself into any river back in Syria. But I will not stick one toe in the Jordan, or take the advice of a man who cannot even be bothered to meet me!'

'Begging your pardon, sir,' mumbled one of Naaman's servants, 'but if the prophet had sent you off to do something hard, you would have gone straight away, wouldn't you?'

'Of course,' grunted Naaman. 'Any soldier would!'

'Well then, why can't you go and do something easy – like washing in the river? It can't hurt, and it just might work!'

Naaman sighed, 'All right,' and led his men to the river.

He dipped himself twice. Nothing.

He dunked himself twice more. His skin was as ugly as ever.

Twice more, and still no cure. Naaman was getting angry again.

But when he came up for the seventh time, spluttering and shaking the water from his face, Naaman's men let out a cheer. Naaman opened his eyes and looked at his hands. The sores were gone! Gone from all over his body.

Naaman dressed and hurried back to Elisha's house. The prophet himself answered the door this time, and Naaman could not contain his joy.

'Take this treasure. Take it all!' Naaman begged. 'For you have saved my life.'

But Elisha said no, for it was God, after all, who had healed Naaman.

'All right, then,' said Naaman, scooping up a pile of earth, 'let me take this with me, so that I can stand on a piece of your land and worship your God too.'

Elisha nodded and smiled.

And God smiled too. For, with a little girl and a muddy river, he had turned an enemy into a friend.

Jonah the Groaner

Jonah was a groaner.

That's right – a groaner.

So when God told him to go to Nineveh and tell the people who lived there to change their evil ways, what did Jonah do?

Jonah groaned.

'Not Nineveh!' he groaned. 'Anywhere but Nineveh. The people who live there are our enemies!'

And when he had stopped groaning, Jonah bought himself a ticket. A ticket for a boat ride. A boat ride that would take him far away from Nineveh.

God listened to Jonah groan. God watched him buy his ticket. But God still wanted Jonah to go to Nineveh.

So when the boat reached the deepest part of the sea, God sent a storm.

'God, help us!' cried a sailor. 'We're sinking!'

'God, save us!' cried another. 'We're tipping over!'

'God must be very angry,' cried the captain, 'with someone here on board.'

And what did Jonah do? Jonah groaned.

'It's me,' Jonah groaned. 'I'm the one God's angry with. He told me to go to Nineveh, and here I am, sailing in the opposite direction. Throw me into the sea and your troubles will be over.'

'God, forgive us!' the sailors cried as they tossed Jonah into the water. And almost at once, the sea grew calm.

'Oh dear,' Jonah groaned, 'I'm sinking.'

'Oh no,' Jonah groaned, 'I'm going to drown.'

'Oh my,' Jonah groaned, 'that's the biggest fish I've ever seen!'

And before he could groan another groan, the fish opened its mouth and swallowed Jonah up!

It was God who sent the fish – to rescue Jonah, and to give him time to think. He had plenty to groan about, of course – the fish's slimy stomach, the seaweed, the smell.

But Jonah was still alive – and that was something to cheer about! So Jonah stopped his groaning and said a prayer:

'I was sinking, Lord. I was drowning. But you saved me. So now I will do whatever you want.'

Three days later, the fish spat Jonah up on a beach. And Jonah kept his promise – he went straight to Nineveh and told the people that God wanted them to change their evil ways.

'Forty days is all you've got,' he warned them. 'And if you haven't changed by then, God will destroy your city.'

The people of Nineveh listened. The people of Nineveh wept. Then the people of Nineveh changed! From the king right down to the poorest slave, they decided to do what was right.

And what did Jonah do? Jonah groaned. He sat himself down in the shadow of a tree, and he groaned.

'I knew this would happen,' he groaned. 'You are a loving God who loves to forgive. But I still don't like the people of Nineveh and I wish they had been destroyed.'

Jonah fell asleep, groaning. And during the night, God sent a worm to kill the tree. When Jonah awoke, he groaned more than ever.

'The tree is dead!' he groaned. 'And now I have no shade.'

'Oh, Jonah,' God sighed. 'You cry about this tree, but you care nothing for the people of Nineveh. I want you to love them like I do.'

'And finally,' God added, 'I want you to stop your groaning!'

Hezekiah Trusts God

Hezekiah was the king of Judah. And he was a good king. He tore down the statues of the false gods and opened up the temple in Jerusalem so his people could worship the true God again.

So God watched over Hezekiah.

When Sennacherib, king of Assyria, sent an enormous army to conquer Jerusalem, God sent an angel who destroyed them all!

Hezekiah was grateful for God's care, but one day Hezekiah fell ill. He lay in his bed, covered with the most awful sores, and with nothing to do but watch the shadow of the sun make its way down the stairs each day.

One step, two steps, three steps, four,

Five steps, six steps, seven steps more,

Eight steps, nine steps, step number ten –

And Hezekiah wondered, 'Will my illness ever end?'

One day a prophet named Isaiah came to visit. At first Hezekiah was glad of his company, but when Isaiah told him the reason for his visit, the king was sorry that he'd ever let him into the palace.

'God has given me a message for you,' said the prophet sadly. 'You will not get better. Do what you must to prepare for your death.'

Without another word, Isaiah left. And the king listened as his footsteps echoed down the stairs.

One step, two steps, three steps, four,

Five steps, six steps, seven steps more,

Eight steps, nine steps, step number ten.

'It's too soon!' sighed Hezekiah. 'Too soon to be the end!'

Hezekiah turned over in his bed, and with his face against the wall, he wept and he prayed: 'Dear God, I have tried to do what is right. And I have always been loyal to you. Do not forget me in my time of need.'

And almost at once, Hezekiah heard footsteps coming up the stairs.

One step, two steps, three steps, four,

Five steps, six steps, seven steps more,

Eight steps, nine steps, step number ten –

It was Isaiah, come to visit again.

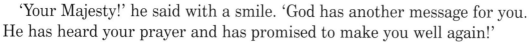

'Your Majesty!' he said with a smile. 'God has another message for you. He has heard your prayer and has promised to make you well again!'

'How can I be sure?' asked the king. 'What sign will God give me?'

'He will make the shadow move ten steps down the stairs,' answered the prophet. 'And then you will know.'

'That happens every day,' said the king. 'And I have watched it – for that is the path the sun travels. But if God should make the shadow go back – back up the stairs, the way the sun never goes – then I will be sure of this sign.'

And so Isaiah prayed. And so God answered. And as Hezekiah watched...

One step, two steps, three steps, four,
Five steps, six steps, seven steps more,
Eight steps, nine steps, step number ten.
The shadow went back up the stairs again!
And Hezekiah – good King Hezekiah – lived
to rule God's people for fifteen years
more!

Down in the Well

Down in the well. Deep down in the well. Deep down in the very bottom of the well, there was no water!

But down in the well. Deep down in the well. Deep down in the very bottom of the well, there were spiders and slugs and slithering snakes – and the prophet Jeremiah.

What was he doing down in the well? Deep down in the very bottom of the well?

He was waiting, that's what, and wondering and wishing for someone to pull him out.

God had whispered in the prophet's ear, you see. And Jeremiah had passed the message on to the king.

'Change your ways! Do what's right! Or I will let your enemies, the Babylonians, conquer your country and turn your people into slaves.'

The king did not want to hear this message. And he didn't want anyone else to hear it, either.

So he had God's messenger, poor Jeremiah, dropped down in the well. Deep down in the well. Deep down in the very bottom of the well.

It was dark down there. Too dark for Jeremiah to see. But it wasn't too dark for God! He saw Jeremiah brush a spider off his face. He watched as the snakes slithered closer.

And then God did something. He whispered into the ear of one of the king's servants, a man called Ebed-Melech. And he told him to go and fetch his dirty laundry!

Down in the well. Deep down in the well. Deep down to the very bottom of the well dropped Ebed-Melech's laundry. And it landed right on Jeremiah's head.

'Hey!' hollered the prophet. 'What's this?'

'My clothes!' called Ebed-Melech. 'Everything but what I'm wearing on my back. I've tied them together like a rope. Now wrap them around you, quickly, and I will pull you out.'

And so, more determined than ever to pass on God's message, the prophet rose up from the well. Right up from the well. Right up from the very bottom of the well.

The Boys Who Liked to Say No

God was very sad. Most of his people had stopped listening to him and talking to him and following his rules.

'Change your ways,' God warned them, 'or you will have to leave this special land I gave you long ago.'

But the people would not listen. So God let their enemies defeat them, and destroy their cities, and carry them hundreds of miles away to be slaves in the land of Babylon.

There were, however, a few of God's people who did not forget him. And among them were four young friends: Daniel, Shadrach, Meshach and Abednego.

These boys were clever and strong. So Nebuchadnezzar, the king of Babylon, decided to treat them well. He gave them soft beds, rich food and an education at his very best school – all in the hope that they would forget about the land they'd left.

But Nebuchadnezzar hadn't reckoned on them being the Boys Who Liked to Say No.

King Nebuchadnezzar's chief servant was put in charge of turning these boys into good Babylonians.

'For dinner tonight,' he announced, 'you will have the following choices from the king's own menu:

'Pink pork sausages. Plump pork chops. And perfect pork pies!'

The king's food looked good. But Daniel, Shadrach, Meshach and Abednego knew it was made from something that God's rules said they

should not eat. The rules they had learned in their own land. The rules their God had given them. The rules and the land and the God they had promised never to forget.

So they turned to the king's servant and together they said, 'NO!'

The servant could not believe it.

'No pink pork sausages?' he asked.

'NO!' said Shadrach. 'But I wouldn't mind a few carrots.'

'No plump pork chops?'

'NO!' said Meshach. 'I'll just have a green salad.'

'And not even one perfect pork pie?'

'NO!' said Abednego. 'But some beans would be lovely.'

'The king will be very angry,' the servant explained. 'If you do not eat this food, you will grow tired and ill. And then the king will punish me. Won't you change your mind, please?'

'NO!' said Daniel. 'But you will not get into trouble, for we will not grow tired and ill. Tell the king that we wish to have a contest. For ten days, the four of us will eat nothing but vegetables and water. The other boys in the palace can eat your food. And then we shall see who is well – and who is not.'

The servant agreed. And so did the king. And for ten days, the Boys Who Liked to Say No said NO to everything but vegetables and water – while the other boys ate their fill of the king's food.

What happened? The God who Daniel, Shadrach, Meshach and Abednego would not forget did not forget them! At the end of the contest, the Boys Who Liked to Say No looked healthy and strong. Much healthier and stronger than the other boys, in fact!

So from then on, Daniel, Shadrach, Meshach and Abednego were allowed to eat whatever they liked. All because they were loyal to their God. And because they were the Boys Who Liked to Say No.

73

The Men Who Liked to Say No

One day, King Nebuchadnezzar's herald announced: 'All wise men and governors must go to the Plain of Dura. The king has a surprise for you!'

When the wise men got there, they found the biggest statue they had ever seen. And at its feet was the biggest band they had ever seen.

'At the sound of the trumpet, the horn, the bagpipe and the harp, you must all bow down and worship this golden statue,' the herald shouted. 'Anyone who disobeys will be thrown into a flaming fiery furnace!'

The band began to play. And everyone worshipped the statue. Well, almost everyone. For there were three men who did not bow down and worship. Shadrach, Meshach and Abednego. All grown up now. The Men Who Liked to Say No.

When King Nebuchadnezzar saw them, he was very angry.

'Who dares defy my order?' he growled.

'Shadrach, Meshach and Abednego,' some men said – men who didn't like foreigners from Jerusalem having such important jobs.

'Bring them to me at once!' growled Nebuchadnezzar.

So the Men Who Liked to Say No were dragged before the king.

'You heard the order,' growled Nebuchadnezzar. 'And you did not obey. Will you worship the statue now?'

'NO!' said Shadrach. 'We will not worship your statue. Our God has told us that this would be wrong.'

'NO!' said Meshach. 'And we will not forget our God, or the land he gave us – the land from which we were taken.'

'NO!' said Abednego. 'And our God will not forget us!'

'Then off to the furnace!' growled the king. 'Make it seven times hotter than it's been before! And tie them up, so they cannot escape!'

So the Men Who Liked to Say No were thrown into the furnace. Its flames were so hot that the men who threw them in were burned up in an instant! But things were different for the three friends. They weren't burning. They weren't sweating. And they weren't alone!

74

There beside them stood an angel, flickering like the furnace flames. He touched a finger to the ropes that bound them and they burned right through. But there wasn't even a blister on the skin of Shadrach, Meshach and Abednego.

'God is with you,' the angel whispered. 'You have nothing to fear.'

Now Nebuchadnezzar's lips were no longer twisted in an angry snarl. No, they hung open and limp with amazement.

'We threw three men into the furnace,' he said. 'But look, there are four men in there now.'

The herald crept closer and said, 'It must be an angel. Sent by the god these men refused to forget. If so, he is a very powerful god, for they are unharmed!'

Nebuchadnezzar leaped to his feet and ordered Shadrach, Meshach and Abednego to come out.

Everyone gathered round them to have a closer look.

And then, the king said: 'Praise be to the God of Shadrach, Meshach and Abednego – the One God! They did not forget him and he did not forget them. I therefore command that no one shall say anything bad about this God. And what is more, I shall give Shadrach, Meshach and Abednego even more important jobs in my kingdom.'

Then he looked at the three friends. 'Surely,' he grinned, 'you can say "Yes" to that?' The three friends looked at each other.

Then, together, they looked at the king.

'NO… problem,' they answered.

Daniel and the Lions

Daniel missed his home in Jerusalem. But he wanted to please God, wherever he was, so he worked hard at the jobs he was given – so hard that he became one of the king's own helpers! But he never forgot about God, or failed to pray to him, morning, noon and night.

Some of the king's men were jealous of Daniel. They wanted his job for themselves. So they talked the king into making a new law – a law which said, 'No one, but no one, is allowed to pray to anyone but the king himself.'

'We've got Daniel now!' his enemies laughed.

And so they had. For the very next morning, Daniel knelt by his window, bowed his head and prayed – not to the king, but to God.

'Thank you for taking care of us in this faraway land,' he prayed. 'Forgive us, and please take us back to our own land soon.'

Daniel's enemies were watching. And before he could even open his eyes, they grabbed him and dragged him in front of the king.

The king was sad. Very sad. He liked Daniel. But he could not break his own law.

'Daniel must be punished,' he sighed. 'Throw him into the lion pit.'

But even as the king gave the order, he whispered a prayer that no one could hear. A prayer to Daniel's God that, somehow, Daniel might be saved.

The pit was dark. The pit was deep. The lions covered its floor like a shaggy growling carpet. They leaped to their feet in a second when Daniel landed among them. They licked their lips. They showed their teeth. Their eyes shone bright and fierce. They opened their mouths and moved towards their dinner. And then they stopped.

'Shoo! Scat! Go away!' shouted a voice right behind Daniel.

The lions' mouths snapped shut. Their tails drooped. And they whimpered away to the corners of the cave.

Slowly Daniel turned around, and looked up into the face of an enormous angel!

'Nothing to worry about now,' the angel smiled. 'God sent me to watch over you. Why don't you get some sleep?'

The next morning, the king cheered when he discovered that Daniel was still alive.

'Pull Daniel out,' he ordered his men. 'And while you're at it, take the men that talked me into that silly law and dump them into the pit instead.'

The king put his arm around Daniel and walked him back to the palace.

Meanwhile Daniel's enemies cried for help. And the lions enjoyed their breakfast!

77

Esther Was a Star

Esther was a star – a beautiful Jewish girl chosen by the king of Persia to be his queen.

Esther had an uncle called Mordecai who was very kind. When Esther's parents died, he raised her as his own daughter. And when she was made queen, he warned her not to tell the king that she had come from one of his captive lands.

And so the king was clueless. He loved Queen Esther, but he did not know she was a Jew.

Haman was horrible. He was the king's right-hand man and he loved nothing as much as pushing people around. One day Haman was walking through the city when he met some of the king's other servants.

'Bow before me!' horrible Haman commanded. And they bowed. All except for Mordecai.

'I will bow before no one but God,' said Mordecai.

Haman was furious, and went straight to the king to seek his revenge.

'There is a troublesome race of people in our land,' he said, 'who worship a different god. They are the Jews, Your Majesty. Give me your permission, and I will do away with them.'

The king was clueless. So he told horrible Haman to kill every Jew in the land – not knowing that he was condemning his own queen!

When Mordecai heard the news he went to see Esther.

'Go to the king,' he said. 'And do what you can to save us!'

'But I have to wait for the king to invite me into his presence,' Esther explained. 'If I go to him without his invitation, the law of the Persians says that he has the right to kill me.'

'You must go anyway,' said Mordecai. 'Whatever the risk. God puts people in places at just the right time, so they can do what he wants. God has put you in the palace to save your people.'

Esther was a star. So Esther went to see the king. And far from being angry, the king was delighted to see her.

'What do you want, my darling?' he asked.

'I want to have a dinner party,' said Esther. 'And I want to invite your right-hand man, Haman.'

The king agreed. The date was set. And horrible Haman was happy. He'd been building a horrible hanging machine in his garden, where he hoped to murder Mordecai. And the queen's invitation made him happier still.

But when he got to the party, horrible Haman was suddenly not so happy.

'I have had some sad news today,' said the queen with tears in her eyes. 'Someone wants to see me dead. And not only me, but all of my people too.'

'Who is this person?' shouted the king. 'Tell me and he will soon be dead instead!'

'There he is,' said Esther. And she pointed at Haman.

'I don't understand.' Haman trembled. 'I have nothing against you.'

'Yes, you do,' said Esther. 'For I am a Jew. And you mean to kill us all!'

The king was no longer clueless. He saw everything clearly now. He loved his queen. He did not care that she was a Jew. But he was very angry with Haman.

'Put him to death,' the king ordered. And so Haman was hanged on his very own hanging machine.

But Esther and Mordecai and all their people lived on – lived on to return to their own land.

And all because Esther was a star!

A Time to Build

'My people have learned their lesson,' God decided. 'It's time for them to come home.'

So God whispered in the ear of Cyrus, king of the country where God's people were slaves. 'Send them home,' God said.

So Cyrus did. And thousands and thousands of people returned to Jerusalem.

There was a lot of work to do when they got there: rebuilding their houses – so they had somewhere to live; rebuilding the temple – so they had somewhere to worship God; rebuilding the walls around Jerusalem – so they had somewhere to hide from their enemies.

It was hard work. They had no end of problems. And for a long time it looked as if it would never be done.

And then Cyrus died. And another king, named Artaxerxes, took his place. And God took the chance to help his people by whispering in the ear of a man who could get *that* king's attention.

The man's name was Nehemiah. His job was to bring the king his wine each day – and to taste it first, to see that no one had put any poison in it! The king trusted him very much, and was puzzled when Nehemiah arrived one day, cup in hand, with a sad frown on his face.

'What's the matter, Nehemiah?' the king asked. 'Why do you look so sad?'

Nehemiah whispered a prayer before he answered.

'Forgive me, Your Majesty,' Nehemiah begged. 'I know it is my duty to smile in your presence, but I cannot. I have heard that my people are suffering in their homeland. The walls of Jerusalem are broken down and I know that I could help, if only I could go and join them.

'I know also that you have wood and stone which would make their job so much easier. Please, send me there with supplies to finish the job and bring an end to my people's suffering.'

King Artaxerxes thought long and hard. 'Yes, Nehemiah,' he answered. 'You may go. But let me send some of my soldiers along to protect you on the way.'

Nehemiah thanked the king. He thanked God too. And he set off on his long journey.

When Nehemiah arrived, he found Jerusalem in a terrible state. But the people were pleased to see him.

'Let's build up these walls,' he encouraged them. 'For God is with us. He gave me courage to speak to the king. He persuaded the king to give us these supplies. And now God will help us finish the job.'

The people cheered and set to work. It still wasn't easy. There were enemies to deal with, so sometimes they had to work with a hammer in one hand and a sword in the other. But finally they finished. The walls were built. Their houses too. And they had even finished the temple, where the people gathered to talk with God.

'Forgive us for not listening to you,' they prayed. 'We promise to do better in the future – to live the way you told us when you gave us this land so long ago. Thank you for giving us another chance, and for bringing us home at last!'

Stories from
The New Testament

The First Christmas

'Good news!' said the angel to a girl named Mary. 'God is sending Someone Special into the world. He will be a great king. His name will be Jesus. And guess what? God wants you to be his mother!'

'Good news!' said the angel to a carpenter named Joseph. 'God is sending Someone Special into the world. He will rescue everyone from the wrong things they have done. He will be God's own Son! But guess what? God wants you to take his mother Mary as your wife, and raise little Jesus as your own.'

'Bad news!' sighed Joseph to Mary. 'The rulers of our country want to count us, to see how many of our people there are. And to make it easier for them, we have to go back to our home town. That means a trip all the way from Nazareth to Bethlehem! And with the baby due so soon…'

'Bad news!' sighed the innkeeper, shaking his head. 'There's not one room left in Bethlehem. But seeing as the young lady's expecting and all, why don't you spend the night in my stable?'

84

'Good news!' smiled Joseph, handing the baby to Mary. 'It's a boy, just as God promised. God's own Son, there in your arms – Jesus.'

'Good news!' called the angel to the shepherds on the hill. 'God has sent Someone Special into the world. The someone you have been waiting for. If you hurry into Bethlehem, you can see him for yourselves. He's just a baby now, wrapped up warmly and lying in a manger. But one day he will save you from all that is wrong. One day he will bring you peace!'

Then the angels filled the sky with a good news song. The shepherds went to Bethlehem and made a good news visit. And, on that very first Christmas Day, Mary just watched, and rocked her baby, and smiled a good news smile!

85

The Wise Men's Visit

The sky was black. The night was clear. The stars were bright as diamonds.

'Perfect,' said the star-watcher. 'Just as it should be.' But just then God nudged the brightest star and sent it floating like a kite across the night sky.

'Quick,' called the star-watcher to his friends. 'Come and see. There's a new star and that means…'

'… a new king!' said the second star-watcher. 'Somewhere a new king is about to be born!'

'I'll tell you what,' said the third star-watcher, 'let's follow the star and see.'

So the three star-watchers climbed onto their camels and set off after the star. When it zigged, they zigged. When it zagged, they zagged – across deserts and mountains and rivers. Until they reached the land of God's people, the Jews.

'We have come a long way,' said the first star-watcher to King Herod.

'We have followed a remarkable star,' added the second star-watcher.

'So can you tell us where the baby is?' asked the third star-watcher. 'The baby born king of the Jews?'

'King of the Jews? King of the Jews?' King Herod repeated, trying hard not to look upset. 'Let me speak with my advisers.'

And so King Herod called a meeting. A meeting that was not very happy.

'King of the Jews?' the king shouted. 'King of the Jews? I AM THE KING OF THE JEWS!!'

'Y-yes, Your Majesty,' his advisers mumbled. 'But God has always promised that one day he would send us a special king.

P-perhaps he is the one the star-watchers are looking for.'

'Hmm,' Herod muttered. 'And where does God say this special king will be born?'

'In Bethlehem, Your Majesty. The city of David.'

'Send for the star-watchers,' King Herod ordered. 'I have decided what I shall do.'

'Gentlemen,' said the king, 'the child you seek is somewhere in Bethlehem. Go to him. Find him. Then come and tell me where he is, so that I can visit him too.'

The king said this with a smile, but his heart was black, black as a night without stars. For he had already determined to kill the child, so no one would take his place as king.

The star-watchers didn't know that when they left, but they soon found out. For the same God who had nudged the star visited them in a dream and told them the king's dark plan.

So they went to see young Jesus, and gave him gifts of gold and frankincense and myrrh. And then they went straight home, with stars in their eyes and God in their hearts.

The Boy in the Temple

'Excuse me,' said Mary, 'but have you seen my boy, Jesus?'

'I'm sorry to trouble you,' said Joseph, 'but I can't seem to find my son. He's twelve and about so tall.'

Again and again they asked, but Mary and Joseph found nothing but shrugs and sympathetic looks and 'Sorry, I can't help you.'

They were worried. They were scared. They didn't know what else to do. And what made it worse was that this should have been such a wonderful trip – off to Jerusalem to visit the Temple and celebrate the Passover holiday. But now they were on their way home – and Jesus was missing!

It was getting dark. 'We've asked everyone we came with,' Mary wept. 'And no one has seen him.'

Joseph snapped his fingers. 'What about those boys? The ones from the next village? Jesus walked with them awhile on the way down here.'

'I've already spoken to them,' sighed Mary, wiping her eyes. 'Nothing.'

'Then there's only one thing left to do,' said Joseph. 'We must go back to Jerusalem and look for him there.'

And so they went, retracing their steps – road by road, street by street, alley by alley, until they arrived, exhausted, at the Temple.

'Have you seen a boy?' said Joseph to one of the Temple priests. 'He's twelve, he's...'

'Have we seen a boy?' the priest grinned. 'We certainly have. His name is Jesus, right?'

'Yes!' cried Joseph. 'But how did you know?'

'Come with me,' the priest chuckled, 'and I'll show you.'

The priest led them to a corner of the Temple courtyard. There was a crowd gathered, listening to one of the Temple teachers. And seated right at the teacher's feet was Jesus!

'The boy is remarkable!' the priest whispered to Joseph. 'He has been going from teacher to teacher, asking the most amazing questions. And when the teachers quiz him, he answers with a wisdom well beyond his years. You should be very proud!'

'I'm certainly amazed,' Joseph sighed. 'But I would be much prouder if he hadn't worried his mother and me half to death. We should be halfway back to Nazareth by now!'

When the teacher had finished, Joseph and Mary rushed straight to Jesus. They hugged him, they led him out of the Temple, but it didn't take long before they told him how they felt.

'What did you think you were doing?' Mary asked. 'We were worried sick!'

'I'm sorry,' Jesus said. 'I thought you'd know where I was.' Then he looked back at the Temple and whispered, 'It is my Father's house, after all.'

Mary and Joseph looked at each other. Jesus took their hands. And together they started off home.

Jesus is Baptized

John was shouting.

John was shouting in the wilderness.

'God is sending Someone Special!' he shouted. 'And you'd better get ready to meet him.'

Many people listened to John. They thought that *he* was Someone Special. He lived in the wilderness, after all, by the River Jordan. He wore a scratchy camel hair shirt. And he ate locusts for lunch!

'I'm not the Special One,' John shouted. 'Why, I'm not even special enough to stoop down and undo his sandals. No, I'm just here to help you get ready to meet him.'

'And how do we do that?' someone shouted back.

'You repent!' John shouted. 'That's how! You stop doing what's bad and you start doing what's good. If you meet a poor man, you don't tell him to go away – you give him food and clothes. If you're a tax collector, you don't take more than you're supposed to – you're honest and kind. And if you're a soldier, you don't bully people – you protect them and take care of them.'

'And what about us?' shouted some Very Religious People.

'You,' John shouted, louder than ever, 'need to stop pretending that

you're perfect – and admit that you have done things that make God sad!
I'll say it again – God is sending Someone Special! And you – all of you –
need to get ready to meet him. So come, let me dip you in this river to
show God that you want your lives to change.'

The people came. John dipped them in the river. And then, one day,
when all the shouting and dipping was done, someone else came too.

It was Jesus. Thirty years old now and all grown up. John recognized
him right away, and stopped his shouting. 'You're the Special One, aren't
you?' he whispered. And Jesus just smiled.

'That's right,' Jesus said. 'And I want you to dip me
too.'

'Oh no,' John said, 'It should be the other way
around!'

'Listen,' said Jesus. 'It's time I began the
work I was sent to do. And this is how my
Father wants me to get started.'

So John agreed, and he and Jesus
waded out into the water. John dipped
Jesus in the river, and when he came
back up again, shaking the wet hair
from his eyes, the clouds parted and
a dove landed on Jesus' shoulder. It
was a sign that God was with Jesus.

'Well done, Son,' God said. 'I'm
proud of you. You really are
Someone Special.'

91

Jesus' Special Friends

Jesus grew up in a place called Galilee, where there was a large and beautiful lake. And it was there that he began the work God gave him to do.

'God is like a king,' he told the people. 'And he wants all of you to be a part of his kingdom – to love him and to love each other.'

People liked to hear Jesus talk. In fact, one morning the crowd was so huge that Jesus was nearly pushed into the sea.

'Excuse me,' Jesus asked a fisherman, 'could I borrow your boat for a while?'

The fisherman's name was Peter. 'Of course,' he said. 'It's doing me no good. I was out all night and didn't catch a thing.'

Jesus climbed into the boat. Peter rowed it a little way from shore. And from there, Jesus talked to the crowd. When he had finished, Jesus sent the people home. And then he turned to Peter.

'Let's go a little further out,' he whispered. 'I'd like to catch some fish.'

Peter tossed back his head and laughed. 'I told you. My men and I were out all night. We caught nothing!'

Jesus didn't say a word. He just smiled and looked across the lake.

'All right,' Peter sighed. 'If that's what you want.'

So Peter sailed to the deepest part of the lake. Then he dropped his fishing nets over the side.

It took no time at all. The nets started pulling and jerking and stretching. And it was all Peter could do to keep the boat from tipping over.

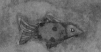

'Help!' Peter
called to some friends
nearby. 'Help me, please!'
And they rowed to him as fast
as they could.

Then, all together, the men pulled on
the nets – and the fish came tumbling and slapping
onto the decks of both boats. Red fish and blue fish. And not just one or
two fish. So many, in fact, that the boats would have sunk had the
fishermen not rowed quickly back to shore.

Peter looked at the fish. Peter looked at his friends. Then Peter looked at
Jesus, and fell to his knees, trembling.

'Only God, or somebody full of his power, could do that,' Peter said. 'And
why would someone like that want to go fishing with the likes of me?'

Jesus shook his head and smiled. 'Don't be scared,' he said. 'God has
given me a lot of work to do. And I need helpers. Helpers like you and your
friends. Once you fished for fish. But from now on, you'll be fishing for
people. And helping me bring them to God.'

Then Jesus stepped out of the boat and walked away, across the shore.
'Come with me,' he called.

Peter and his friends watched him go. They looked at the fish. They
looked at each other. Then they dropped their nets, left their boats behind,
and raced off to follow Jesus.

Down Through the Roof

Anna stuck a finger through the hole in her skirt.

'How did that get there?' she wondered.

She would have run to her mother to have it mended, but her mother was on the other side of the house. And the house was full.

Packed full.

Jammed full.

Chock-a-block full.

Why? Because Jesus was visiting.

The old man and woman standing in front of Anna shifted, and she squeezed into the hole between them. She could see better now.

Jesus was a lot like her father. They both taught people about God. They both prayed beautiful prayers. But Jesus could do something else. Something her father had never done. Jesus could make sick people well! No wonder the whole town had crowded into her house.

Suddenly something dropped on Anna's head.

Anna looked up. And there was another hole – a hole in the roof!

Anna stepped back.

The hole got bigger.

The crowd stepped back.

And the hole got bigger still.

'What's going on up there?' shouted Anna's father. And, instead of an answer, a man dropped through the hole. A man lying on a mat with a rope at each corner. A poor, sick man who could not even move. His friends lowered him carefully to the floor, and Jesus gently laid a hand on his head.

'My friend,' Jesus said, 'the wrong things you have done are now forgiven.'

'Wait a minute!' growled Anna's father. 'Wait just a minute. Only God can take away someone's sins. Just who do you think you are?'

'Oh dear,' thought Anna. Her father often got angry when he talked with people about God.

But Jesus wasn't angry at all. 'Which is easier?' he said calmly. 'To forgive a lame man's sins, or to make him walk?'

It was all Anna could do not to giggle. 'What a silly question,' she thought. 'One is just as hard as the other!'

'Well,' Jesus continued. 'To show you that God has given me the power to fix what is wrong in this man's heart, I shall fix what is wrong with his legs.'

'Stand up!' Jesus ordered the man. 'You can do it.'

And the man did!

What is more, he rolled up the mat, slung it over his shoulder and walked out through the front door.

His friends climbed down from the roof to join him. The crowd followed behind, cheering. But all Anna could do was stare up through that hole and smile!

The Centurion's Servant

The Roman centurion stood before his soldiers. There were a hundred in all, each and every man sworn to do whatever the centurion commanded.

'Fetch my sword,' he ordered.

'Yes, sir! Right away, sir!' shouted one of the soldiers. And he was off in a flash.

'Fetch my shield!' he added.

'Yes, sir! Right away, sir!' And another soldier ran off as well.

'Forward march!' he shouted once everything was ready.

'Yes, sir! Right away, sir!' answered each and every man. And they marched off together through the streets of Capernaum.

The centurion was used to giving orders. And he was used to being obeyed. Not only by his men, but by the people of Capernaum as well. For the Romans were in charge of that city and all the land where Jesus lived – a land they had taken by force and now ruled with a cruel hand.

One day, the centurion went home to hear some bad news. His servant was ill – unable to move and in great pain. The centurion felt sorry for his servant, but for all his power, there was nothing he could do, no order he could give, to make that pain go away.

So the centurion went to see Jesus. He'd heard that Jesus made sick people well, and so his request was simple.

'Help me sir,' he said. 'My servant is terribly ill.'

The people standing round Jesus wondered what he would do. This centurion and his soldiers had bullied them and stolen from them and pushed them around. Would Jesus do for this man what he had for so many others?

But there was no question in Jesus' mind. He had taught his followers to love everyone, even their enemies. How could he do any less?

'I will go and heal him,' he said.

And then the centurion said something that surprised them all.

'No,' he said. And could it be that he was remembering all the cruel things he had done? 'I do not deserve to have you visit my house. But I do know this. I am a man with power and authority. I tell my soldiers to fetch this and they do it, saying, "Yes, sir! Right away, sir!" I tell them to fetch something else, and the answer is the same. "Yes, sir! Right away, sir!" And when I order them to march, they obey. "Yes, sir! Right away, sir!"

'You have power too, power over sickness. So all you need to do is give the order and I know that my servant will be healed.'

Jesus turned to those around him, amazed. 'This man trusts me, he really does! I have not found this kind of trust even among our own people. And I'm telling you the truth when I say that people just like this man – people from all over the world – will one day be a part of all that God is doing. But, because they do not trust me, some of our own people will miss out.'

Then he turned to the centurion and said, 'Go. All that you hope for will happen.'

And at that very hour, the centurion's servant was healed.

'Yes, sir! Right away, sir!'

The Storm on the Lake

It was a perfect day.

The sky was blue. The lake too.

And a gentle breeze whipped the wave tips white and foamy.

Jesus sat at the side of the lake and talked to the people about God.

'God is your Father,' he said. 'He dresses the flowers in beautiful colours. He makes sure the birds have enough to eat. But you are his sons and his daughters. Don't you think he can clothe and feed you too? So trust him, and stop worrying your lives away.'

When Jesus had finished teaching, he was tired. So he called his closest friends, and together they piled into a boat and set off across the lake for home.

Jesus yawned. He stretched. He laid his head down and, to the rhythm of the waves and the rocking of the boat, he fell asleep. It was the perfect end to a perfect day!

And then, suddenly, the day was not so perfect.

The sky turned black. The lake too.

And a wild wind stirred the waves up tall and stormy.

The boat rocked right. The boat rocked left. The boat rocked up and down. The boat rocked so hard, in fact, that Jesus' friends were sure they would all drown.

But Jesus slept right through it – except for the odd snuffle and snore.

'Jesus!' his friends called at last. 'Jesus! Wake up! We're all going to drown!'

So Jesus woke
up. Then he sat up. Then
he rubbed his eyes and he stood up.
It was all anybody else could do to stay on their feet. But
Jesus stood up! And then, very calmly, he said to the wind,
'Quiet now.' And he said to the waves, 'Settle down.'

And they did!

Then Jesus turned to his friends and said, 'You didn't need to be
frightened. You didn't have to worry. All you had to do was trust me.
See, everything is calm.'

And so it was. The sky was blue. The lake too. And the little waves
splashed happily at the side of the boat.

It was a perfect day again!

'Time to Get Up'

'Jesus! Help me, Jesus! My daughter is dying!' Jairus shouted as loud as he could, and the crowd parted to let him through.

'She's only twelve,' he explained. 'And she's so ill. But I know I can count on you to make her well. Please!'

Jesus nodded. 'Show me the way,' he said. But the minute they started wading through the crowd, Jesus stopped.

'Somebody touched me,' he whispered.

'Jesus,' one of his friends whispered back, 'there are hundreds of people here. I'm sure lots of them touched you.'

'No,' said Jesus, raising his voice now. 'Somebody here was sick. Very sick. Then they touched me and God made them well. I felt it. I felt the power rush out of me! Now, who was it?'

'It was me,' said a woman close by. 'I have been sick for so long. I've spent so much money on doctors. But when I touched your robe, I was healed!'

Jesus turned to the woman and smiled. He was so happy for her. 'You trusted me,' he said. 'That's good. So God has made you well.'

'Jesus,' said Jairus. 'Jesus, I don't mean to interrupt...'

But before Jairus could say another word, one of his servants called out across the crowd, 'Master, master, I have the most awful news...'

Jairus knew it even before the servant spoke.

'... your daughter is dead.'

Jesus turned from the happy woman to the sad father.

'It will be all right,' he said. 'Trust me.' Then they hurried off to Jairus' house.

When they arrived, there was another crowd – wailing and weeping in front of the house. The sad news had spread fast.

'Listen, everybody,' said Jesus. 'There's no need to cry. The girl is not dead. She's only sleeping.'

Sad tears gave way to angry laughter. 'Don't be ridiculous!' someone shouted. 'We've seen her. She's dead!'

Jesus ignored them all. He asked the girl's mother and father, and three of his friends, Peter, James and John, to come with him. Together they walked straight to where the girl was lying.

She certainly looked dead. Her eyes were closed. Her face was pale. Her skin was cold. But that didn't stop Jesus. He took her cold hand in his and called, 'Little girl, little girl, it's time to get up.'

Her skin grew warm. Her face flushed pink. And her eyelids flickered and flew open. She was alive!

And the first thing she said was, 'I'm hungry!'

'Then we'd better get you something to eat,' said Jesus.

And it was the best meal that family ever had.

The Marvellous Picnic

It wasn't long before lots of people wanted to hear Jesus talk about God. And many more wanted him to make them well. So they followed him everywhere. From town to town. From city to country. And all the way back again.

'We need a rest,' Jesus said to his friends one day. So they took a little boat trip across Lake Galilee, hoping to camp for a while in the hills beyond. But the people were so eager to see Jesus that they raced around the shoreline to meet him on the other side!

Jesus was tired. But when he turned and saw the people following him up the hill, he stopped. 'They're like sheep without a shepherd,' he said to his friends. 'They need someone to show them the way.'

So he sat himself down – right then and there. And he started to teach.

'God loves you,' Jesus said. 'He knows what's best for you. The most amazing things can happen when you trust him.'

Jesus said a lot more than that. He taught all day, in fact. And by then, the people were hungry.

'Philip!' Jesus called to one of his friends. 'Can you go out and buy some food for these people?'

Philip just laughed. 'There are more than five thousand of them! It would take six months' pay to feed them all.'

Then Andrew, Peter's brother, spoke up. 'There's a boy here, Jesus, who has a little food. Five loaves of bread and a couple of fish. It's not much, but it's a start.'

'So it is,' grinned Jesus, and he rubbed his hands together, as if he were about to go to work. 'Make the people sit down in little groups. Tell them we're going to have a picnic!'

Jesus' friends looked at Jesus. They looked at the boy's little lunch. They looked at the enormous crowd. Then they looked at each other and shrugged.

'All right,' they agreed. 'Whatever you say.'

Jesus smiled as he watched them go. Then he bowed his head, thanked God for the food, and started breaking it into pieces. The friends returned and began to pass out the pieces. And, to their amazement, there was plenty for the first group, and the second group, and the third group, and then every group! Plenty for everyone. More than enough to go around. So much, in fact, that there were twelve baskets full of leftovers to take home!

The people patted their tummies. They struggled to their feet. They wiped the crumbs from their mouths. And some even burped!

But all Jesus' friends could do was stare.

'It's just as I told you,' said Jesus. 'God can do the most amazing things. All we have to do is trust him.'

Then he smiled at his helpers, popped a chunk of bread into his mouth and started off for home.

The Kind Stranger

Jesus was teaching one day when a man in the crowd asked him a question.

'Can you tell me, Jesus, what I have to do to live forever?'

Jesus smiled. 'Love God,' he answered, 'and love your neighbour as much as you love yourself.'

'But who is my neighbour?' asked the man, hoping to trick Jesus. 'Is he just the fellow who lives next door?'

'Let me tell you a story,' Jesus said, 'and I think you will understand.'

'Once upon a time, there was a man – a man like any one of us – who was travelling from Jerusalem to Jericho. Now as you all know, that is a very dangerous road. It's twisty and it's steep, and there's no end of places for robbers and thieves to hide.

'Well, the robbers were waiting that day. And they grabbed the man. And they beat him. And they took his money and left him to die.'

'Oh dear,' sighed the crowd. They felt sorry for the man.

Jesus went on with his story.

'In a little while, another man came walking down that road – a priest, on his way home from worshipping God at the Temple. He saw the dying man, and what do you think he did?'

'He helped him!' shouted someone in the crowd.

'He saved him!' shouted another.

'No!' said Jesus, firmly. 'He did not. He took one look at that poor, beaten man, then crossed to the other side of the road and walked away.'

'Oh my,' the crowd murmured.

'Wait,' Jesus continued. 'Soon another man passed by. He served God at the Temple too. So what do you think this man did when he saw the wounded traveller?'

'He ran for help!' shouted someone.

'He raised the alarm!' shouted another.

'No!' said Jesus, again. 'He did not. Just like the priest, he crossed to

104

the other side of the road and left that poor man to die.'

'Oh no,' the crowd sighed.

'Don't worry,' said Jesus. 'For there was one more man who passed by that day. And he was a Samaritan.'

'A Samaritan?' shouted someone. 'They're different from us!'

'We hate Samaritans!' shouted another.

'And they hate us!' added a third.

'So I've heard,' nodded Jesus. 'But when this Samaritan saw the man, he did not walk away. No. He bandaged his wounds. He loaded him on his donkey. He took him to a nearby inn. And he paid for that man to stay there until he was well.'

Jesus looked at the man who had asked him the question. 'So tell me,' he said, 'which of these men was a neighbour to the man who had been robbed?'

'The third one. The Samaritan,' the man answered.

'That's right,' Jesus smiled. 'Because my neighbour is anyone who needs my help. Now you go and help your neighbour too.'

The Two Sisters

'It's not fair!' moaned Martha. 'It's just not fair! I've cleaned the house from top to bottom. Scrubbed the floor till my fingers hurt. But all my sister Mary does is sit there – sit and talk to Jesus.'

'It's not right!' moaned Martha. 'It's just not right! I've plucked the chickens and baked the bread and sweated for hours over a hot stove. But all my sister Mary does is sit there – sit and talk to Jesus.'

'It won't do!' moaned Martha. 'It just won't do! Mopping up. Washing up. Tidying up. I've done it all and I'm fed up! Because all my sister Mary does is sit there – sit and talk to Jesus.'

'Martha,' sighed Jesus. 'Martha, my friend. I'm so glad you invited me to your house. The place is spotless. The food was delicious. But you mustn't be angry with Mary your sister. For she has made the right choice.

'Cooking and cleaning and washing up are important. But sometimes it's better to put away your brushes and cloths. To rest. And to sit and talk with me.'

The Unforgiving Servant

Peter asked Jesus a question.

'If somebody hurts me,' he said, 'and then says, "I'm really sorry", how many times should I forgive him and say, "Hey, that's OK"?'

Before Jesus could answer, however, Peter offered an answer of his own.

He thought it would sound good.

He thought it would sound big-hearted.

He thought it would be the kind of thing Jesus would like to hear.

'Should I forgive him… seven times?' he said.

It seemed like a lot of times to Peter. But Jesus was not impressed.

'No,' answered Jesus. 'Not seven times. But seventy TIMES seven times!'

Peter did some quick sums. That was a lot of times. A whole lot of times! More times than Peter had ever forgiven anybody.

So Jesus told him a story.

'Once there was a king. And one of his servants owed him money.

Not a little money. Not lots of money. But loads and loads and loads of money – millions and millions and more!

One day the servant was brought before the king. And because he could not pay what he owed, the king commanded that the man and his family should be sold as slaves.

The servant fell to his knees.

"I'm really sorry!" he cried. "Be patient with me, please. Just give me another chance. And I promise I will pay back everything I owe."

The king looked at his servant. He felt sorry for

108

him. And then, much to the servant's surprise, the king smiled and said, "Hey, that's OK." Then he called off the debt, and set him free!

The servant left the palace, celebrating. And that's when he ran into another servant – a servant who owed HIM money.

Not loads of money. Not a lot of money, either. A couple of coins – that's all.

Did the first servant remember what the king had done for him? Not for a minute. He grabbed the second servant by the throat and demanded to be paid.

So the second servant fell to his knees.

"I'm really sorry!" he cried. "Be patient with me, please. Give me another chance and I will pay back everything I owe."

But instead of saying, "Hey, that's OK," the first servant had the second servant thrown into jail!

Word of this got back to the king. And he was so angry that he had the first servant dragged before him again.

"When you came to me and said, 'I'm really sorry,' I called off your debt and said, 'Hey, that's OK.' Why couldn't you do the same?"

And with that, the king had the servant thrown into jail until he could repay what he owed.'

Jesus looked at his friend. 'God is like that king. "I'm really sorry." That's what we say to him – more times than we can count. And even more times than that, he tells us "Hey, that's OK." And all he really wants is for us to tell that to each other too.'

'I'm really sorry,' said Peter. 'I didn't understand.'

And Jesus just smiled and said, 'Hey, that's OK.'

'I Can See!'

'I have a question,' said one of Jesus' friends. 'There's a man here who's been blind since he was born. Did that happen because his parents did something bad?'

'No,' said Jesus. 'God doesn't punish people by making their children blind. But I'll tell you what – God can use this man's blindness to show us how powerful he is.'

And with that, Jesus walked over to the man. He knelt down. He spat on the ground. He made a little mud out of the dirt and spit. And he rubbed it on the blind man's eyes. It was very messy!

'Now go and wash your face,' Jesus said to the man. 'And you will be blind no more.'

The man washed his face, just as Jesus said. And when he shook the water from his hair and opened his eyes – he could see!

'We have a question,' said the people who gathered around him. 'Aren't you the blind man who usually goes begging for food?'

'I am,' said the man-who-used-to-be-blind.

'Then how can you see?'

'I met a man named Jesus, who rubbed mud in my eyes!'

The crowd was amazed. They were ready to cheer.

And then someone else spoke up, 'Excuse me. I have a question too.'

This someone was a religious teacher who didn't much like Jesus. Why? Because Jesus was too popular and didn't always agree with what the other teachers said.

'Jesus healed you? And he did it today?' the teacher asked.

'That's right,' said the man.

'Well, today is the day of rest – the special day God himself set aside. The day on which no one is allowed to work. But healing is work, surely! So how can this Jesus be on God's side if he breaks God's law?'

'I don't know,' said the man. 'But I can see!'

'Because a bad man made you well!' accused the teacher.

'Wait,' asked someone else. 'How could a bad man do a good thing like that?'

'That's what I want to know,' said another. And they asked the man-who-used-to-be-blind all kinds of questions.

'Were you really blind?'

'Were you pretending?'

'Who is this Jesus, anyway?'

It was too much for the man-who-used-to-be-blind. 'Listen,' he shouted, 'I don't know the answers to all your questions, but I do know this. Once I was blind, and now I can see. Who but someone sent by God could do a thing like that?'

A little later, as the man was sitting by himself, Jesus came to see him.

'I know it's been a hard day,' said Jesus, 'but I have a question too. Do you believe that God sent me?'

'I do,' said the man. 'I really do!'

Jesus smiled. 'Then no more questions.'

The Two Houses

'Let me tell you a story,' said Jesus to the crowd one day.
'A story all about building.'

'There once was a man. A wise man, who wanted to build a house.
So he found a big rock. A really big rock. And he said, "This is
where I'll start."

And he dug a big hole in that really big rock, and that's
where he built his house.

Then the rain came.

And the sea rose.

And the wind huffed and puffed enough to blow that
house down.

But that house did not move. No, not one inch!

There was another man. A foolish man, who wanted to build a house too.

So he found a nice beach. A soft, sandy beach.

And he said, "This is where I'll start."

And he smoothed out the sand and tossed out the shells. And that's where he built his house.

Then the rain came.

And the sea rose.

And the wind huffed and puffed enough to blow that house down.

And down it fell – with a shiver and a rumble and a crash!

'Listen to my words,' said Jesus. 'Do what I tell you. And you will be like that first man. For the things I say are true – solid as any rock. And you can build your life upon them.'

The Big Party

'Come to my party!' a man said to Jesus. So Jesus went along.

But in the middle of the party, he turned to the man and said, 'You have invited all the wrong people.'

The man was surprised. 'What do you mean?' he asked.

Jesus looked around the room. 'When you throw a party, you invite your important friends, your favourite relatives and your rich neighbours, don't you?'

'Of course,' the man nodded.

'And when they throw a party, you hope they invite you too.'

'That's right,' said the man.

'Well, I have a better idea,' said Jesus. 'The next time you throw a party, send your invitations to the poor, the crippled, the sick and the blind.'

'But why?' asked the man, more confused than ever.

'Because none of those people could ever pay you back. They are not rich enough or well enough to throw parties of their own. But I tell you, God will be so happy with your kindness, that he will save a special seat for you at the party he plans to throw in heaven.'

One of the other guests heard this and shouted, 'Hooray for God and for everybody who gets to go to his party in heaven!'

'That reminds me of a story,' said Jesus.

'Once upon a time, there was a man – a rich man – who threw a big party for his friends. When everything was ready – the drinks and the cakes and the decorations – he told his servant to go and fetch the guests.

When the servant knocked at the first guest's house, the man met him at the door with a worried face.

"I cannot come," he said, "for I have just bought a piece of land and must go and see that it is all right."

When the servant knocked at the second guest's door, the man's face was much the same.

"Cows," said the man. "I've just bought some cows. One can't be too careful with cows. I must make sure they are well."

It was just the same with the third guest.

"Can't come tonight," he explained. "Haven't you heard? I've just got married!"

When the servant reported all this to his master, the rich man was very angry.

"So they can't be bothered to come? Well, I know plenty of people who will. Go out into the streets," he ordered his servant. "And invite the poor, the crippled, the sick and the blind."

And so they came – the people no one else would invite. And it was the best party that rich man ever threw!'

Jesus looked around the room again. 'Hooray for God!' he said. 'Rich and poor. Sick and well. He loves us all. And he wants us all to come to his party.'

The Good Shepherd

When Jesus talked, everybody came to listen.

People who thought they were good.

And people who weren't so good, too – cheats and liars, robbers and thieves.

The people who thought they were good didn't like this one bit.

'Hey, Jesus!' they shouted.

'You say you come from God. You call him your Father. So why are you spending your time with these bad people?'

Jesus thought for a minute. 'Let me tell you a story,' he said.

'Once upon a time, there was a shepherd. A shepherd who had a hundred sheep.

He knew each of them by sight.

The white ones and the black ones.

The spotted ones and the striped ones.

The thin ones and the fat ones.

The sleek ones and the woolly ones.

And every night, after he had called them from the fields and gathered them in their pen, he would count them.

One, two, three.

Four, five, six.

Seven, eight, nine.

And all the way to a hundred.

One night, he found himself a sheep short.

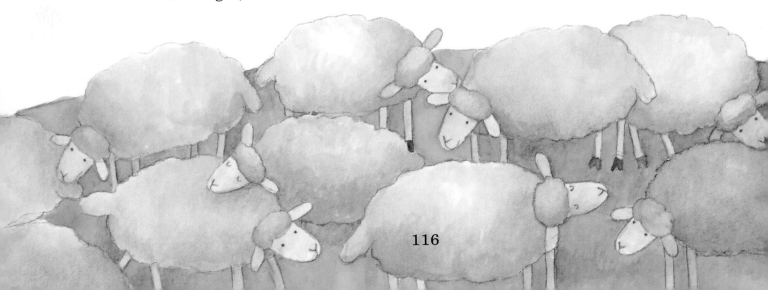

Ninety-seven, ninety-eight, ninety-nine, he counted.

But he never got to a hundred, because the last sheep was missing!

The shepherd looked round the pen. "It's Bramble!" he said. "It's Bramble that's gone." And what do you think he did?

Did he say to himself, "I have ninety-nine sheep left, who cares if one is lost?" Of course not. He cared for the missing sheep as much as for the rest. So he picked up his walking stick and off he went, across the hills and fields, looking for that lost sheep.

He looked under bushes.

He looked behind rocks.

He looked down in deep ravines.

And finally, when he had almost given up hope, he found the lost sheep, trapped in a tangle of thorns.

The shepherd shouted "Hooray!"

Then he slung the sheep round his shoulders, and carried it safely home.

"Come to my house!" he called to his neighbours.

"Come to my house!" he called to his friends.

"My sheep was lost, and now it's found. We're going to have a party!"

'Why do I talk to people who have done bad things?' said Jesus to the crowd. 'Because God is like that shepherd. And we are all his sheep. Some stay in the pen. But some, like these robbers and thieves, wander away and get lost. So someone has to look for them and talk to them. And when they come back to him, God throws a party too!'

The Lost Coin

'Let me tell you another story,' said Jesus to the crowd.

'Once upon a time, there was a woman. A woman who worked very hard.
She worked so hard, in fact, that she managed to save ten days' pay! And she
tucked it away in the safest place in her house.

One, two, three…
Four, five, six…
Seven, eight, nine…
Ten coins in all!
She knew them all by sight.
The shiny ones and the dull ones.
The thick ones and the thin ones.
The smooth ones and the dented ones.
One day, she took them out to count them.
One, two, three…
Four, five, six…
Seven, eight, nine…
But she never got to ten, because the last coin was missing!
The woman looked again inside her little box. "It's the tiny silver one,"
she said. "It's gone!" And what do you think she did?
Did she say to herself, "I have nine coins left, who cares if one is lost?"
Of course not.
She wanted that last coin as much as the rest. So she lit a lamp and
started to look.

She looked under tables and beds and chairs.
She looked under pots and pans.
She reached into crevices, cracks and nooks.
And finally she found it! Nestling in a dark corner.
The woman shouted, "Hooray!"
Then she picked up the coin and danced around the room.
"Come to my house!" she called to her neighbours.
"Come to my house!" she called to her friends.
"My coin was lost and now it's found. We're going to have a party!"

'And that's just what the angels do,' said Jesus, 'when someone who is far away from God turns around and does what is right.'

119

The Big Spender

The people who thought they were good were still not happy with Jesus. They moaned. They grumbled. They frowned.

'It's not fair,' they complained. 'Jesus spends all his time with the bad people.'

Jesus heard this and told them one more story:

'Once upon a time there was a man who had two sons. He loved them both, very much. But one day, the younger son came to him with a sad request.

"Father," the younger son said, "when you die, I will get part of your money and part of your land. The problem is, I don't want to wait. I want my money now!"

It was all the father could do to hold back his tears. But because he loved his son, he agreed, and gave him his share of the money.

That very day the son left home, money in his pocket and a big smile on his face. He didn't even say goodbye. The father just watched, wiped away a tear, and hoped that one day he would see his son again.

The son travelled to a country far, far away and spent his money just as fast as he could. He drank. He gambled. He used his money to do many bad things – until finally the money was gone.

The son looked for a job, but the only work he could find was taking care of pigs! It was hard, dirty work, and he was so hungry sometimes that he thought about taking the pigs' food for himself. He was miserable, lonely and sad. And then one day, he had an idea.

"The servants who take care of my father's animals are much happier than me. I'll go home, that's what I'll do. I'll tell my father how sorry I am for wasting his money. And maybe, just maybe, he'll let me become a servant and work for him."

Now what do you think the father had been doing all this time? Did he say to himself, "I have my eldest son at home with me. Who cares if my younger son is gone?" Of course not! He loved his son, even though he had

120

gone far away. And every day, he would go out to the roadside and watch, hoping his son would return.

That's exactly where he was when the younger son hobbled home, poor and hungry. The father ran to his son and hugged him tight. And the son dropped right to his knees.

"Oh, Father," he cried. "I'm so sorry. I have wasted all your money and am no longer good enough to be your son."

"Don't be silly," said his father. "You are my son. You will always be my son. And I am so glad to have you back!" Then the father lifted his son to his feet and walked him home. He dressed him in beautiful clothes. He put gold rings on his fingers. And he threw him a big welcome-home party.

When the elder son came home from work that night, he heard the party noise.

"What's happening?" he asked. And when a servant told him, he was filled with anger and ran to his father.

"It's not fair!" he shouted. "I've been a good son. I've worked hard for you all these years. But he was bad. He wasted your money. And now you're throwing him a party."

"I love you, my son," the father said. "And you have enjoyed all the good things I have. But your brother was gone, and now he's back. He was lost, and now he's found. That's why I'm having this party, because we're all back together again." '

Big Bags of Money

Here is another story Jesus told.

'Once there was a man with money.

Mounds of money! Mountains of money! More money than you could imagine!

One day, the man decided to take a long trip. So he called three of his servants together and told them what he wanted them to do with his money while he was gone.

The first servant was the hardest worker of them all. So the man said to him, "Here are five big bags of my money. Use them wisely. We'll see how well you've done when I return."

The second servant was a hard worker too. So the man said to him, "Here are two big bags of my money. Use them wisely. We'll see how well you've done when I return."

But the third servant was not a hard worker at all. In fact, he was rather lazy. So the man gave him just one big bag of money. "Use it wisely," he said. "We'll see how well you've done when I return."

So the man with money went away. And after a long, long time, he came back again.

"Tell me," he said to the first servant. "How did you get on? What did you do with my money?"

"You gave me five big bags of money," said the first servant. "I put them to work. I used them to do lots of good things. And look! I made five more big bags of money!"

"Ten bags altogether!" exclaimed the man with money. "Well done! You showed me I could trust you and now I have much bigger things for you to do!"

"And what about you?" said the man with money to the second servant. "How did you get on? What did you do with my money?"

"You gave me two big bags of money," said the second servant. "I put them to work as well. I used them to do lots of good things. And look! I made two more big bags of money!"

"Four bags altogether!" exclaimed the man with money. "Excellent! And now I have a better job for you as well."

Finally, the man with money turned to the third servant.

"And how did you get on?" he asked.

The third servant hummed and hawed and looked at his feet.

"Well, sir," he said. "I know how much you like your money and how disappointed you'd be if I lost it. So I just dug a hole and buried it in the ground. You gave me one big bag of money, so here is your great big bag of money back."

The man with money was furious.

"Don't blame this on me!" he shouted. "I gave you that money to use – to put to work – so that you could make more. And you just couldn't be bothered. Stuck it in a hole? If you'd taken the time to stick it in the bank, it would at least have made a little interest!

"Get out of my sight, you lazy man. You're sacked!"

And he took that servant's bag of money and gave it to the first servant.

So off they went – the man with money and his two hard working servants – off to bigger and better things.

And the third servant? He walked sadly away – in search of another job.'

The Man Who Came Back

One, two, three,
  Four, five, six,
  Seven, eight, nine,
  And ten.
There were ten lepers on the road one day. And no one would go near them. Their fingers were numb. Their faces were scarred. They were terribly, terribly ill.

  One, two, three,
  Four, five, six,
  Seven, eight, nine,
  And ten.
There were ten lepers on the road one day. And Jesus came walking by. 'Jesus!' they cried. 'Oh, Jesus!' they begged. 'Save us. Please make us well!'

  One, two, three,
  Four, five, six,
  Seven, eight, nine,
  And ten.
There were ten lepers on the road one day. And Jesus prayed for them. 'Now go!' he said. 'Go. Find a priest, and he'll tell you if you are well.'

  One, two, three,
  Four, five, six,
  Seven, eight, nine,
  And ten.

There were ten lepers on the road that day. And then suddenly there weren't! Their fingers were fine. Their faces like new! They were happy and healed and whole!

One, two, three,
Four, five, six,
Seven, eight,
And nine.

Nine lepers (who weren't lepers any more!) rushed off to share their good news. But leper number ten went straight back to Jesus, to thank him for what he had done.

One, two, three,
Four, five, six,
Seven, eight, nine,
And ten.

'I healed ten lepers on the road today,' said Jesus to the man. 'But where are the rest? Never mind, I'm just pleased that you came back to thank me!'

The Pharisee and the Tax Collector

There were some very religious people who thought they were better than everyone else. So Jesus told them a story.

'Two men went to the Temple to pray. One was a religious leader – a Pharisee. And the other was a tax collector.
   The Pharisee stood up to pray. He looked straight up to heaven. And this is what he said:
   "Thank you, God, that I am better than other people.
   "Better than robbers.
   "Better than villains.

"Better than those who cheat on their husbands and wives.

"And most definitely better than that tax collector. Everyone knows he's greedy and dishonest. But I keep every religious rule and give away a tenth of all I have."

The tax collector stood up too. But he looked down, down at the ground. He beat his chest in sorrow and shame. And this is what he said:

"I've done lots of bad things. Please, God, forgive me." '

Jesus looked at the religious people. 'So which man did God listen to?' he asked. 'Whose prayer did he answer? The second man, that's who. God forgave every bad thing the man had ever done.

'Remember, if you act as if you're better than other people, then God will put you in your place. But if you're honest about who you are and what you need, then God will put things right!'

Jesus and the Children

'I can't see!' called a blind woman. 'Can you help me, Jesus?'

'I can't walk!' called a lame man. 'Heal me, Jesus, please!'

'He can't hear!' called a deaf man's friend. 'Touch him, Jesus, and make him well.'

They were everywhere – people with every kind of sickness. And Jesus felt sorry for them all. So he did what he could to help the crowd that day.

'I can't see,' said a little girl to her mother. 'There are too many people in the way.'

'I can't move,' said her little brother. 'We're all squashed together.'

'What did you say?' asked their father. 'I can't hear. This crowd is so noisy!'

'Excuse me,' said their mother to one of Jesus' friends. 'We were wondering if Jesus could pray for our children.'

'Are they sick?' asked the friend.

'No,' the mother answered. 'We just wanted Jesus to ask God to watch over them and protect them.'

'I see,' said the friend impatiently. 'Well, as you must have noticed, Jesus is a very busy man. He has important things to do. Lots of sick people to make well.'

'That's right!' added another of Jesus' friends. 'There are grown-ups here who need his help. He can't be bothered with children.'

'Particularly children who aren't even sick!' chimed in a third friend. 'It's just a waste of his time.'

The mother and the father and the children looked at each other. Then they looked at the ground and turned to leave. They were sad and embarrassed.

'Does this mean we won't see Jesus?' asked the little girl, rubbing the tears from her eyes.

But before her mother could answer, another voice

called out across the crowd. 'Wait!' It was the voice of Jesus!

'Bring your children here,' Jesus called. 'There's nothing to be ashamed of.' And he gave his friends an unhappy look.

Jesus picked up the little boy and the little girl and put them on his lap. He gave them each a hug, and then he said, 'Listen. I want everybody to listen. Particularly my friends. You must never keep the children away from me. They are as important to me as anyone else. And I want to be their friend too.

'Don't you see? God wants us all to be like these children. To love him like a father. To trust him completely. And to long to be with him.'

Then Jesus prayed for the children, hugged them one more time and sent them beaming back to their parents.

Jesus and the Taxman

'Jesus is coming!' somebody shouted. 'Jesus is coming to Jericho!' And everybody ran to meet him.

Well, almost everybody. For there was one man – one wee little man – who did not run to meet Jesus. And his name was Zacchaeus.

It's not that Zacchaeus didn't want to see Jesus. He did. He really did. But, not only was Zacchaeus short, he was also afraid of the crowd. Not many people liked him, you see. Partly because he was a tax collector. But mostly because he collected more taxes than he was supposed to – and kept what was left for himself.

'Jesus is here!' somebody shouted. 'Jesus is here in Jericho!' And everybody cheered as he walked through the city gates.

Well, almost everybody. For Zacchaeus did not feel like cheering at all. He wanted to see Jesus. He really did. But how could he walk out there in front of all those people he'd cheated? And what would they do if they got hold of him?

Then Zacchaeus had an idea. There were trees by the city gates – tall, leafy trees. If he could sneak behind the crowd and climb one of those trees, he could see Jesus – and not be seen himself!

So off he went – out of his house and through the empty streets. And because the crowd was watching Jesus, he had no trouble at all slipping behind them and shinning up a tree.

'Come, eat at my house!' somebody shouted. 'Come, eat at my house, Jesus!' And because it was a great honour to host someone as important as Jesus, everybody shouted at once.

Well, almost everybody.

130

For there was one man – one wee little man – who kept his mouth shut and tried hard not to rustle the branches.

'Thank you very much,' said Jesus. 'You are very kind. But I have already decided where I will eat my dinner.'

Then Jesus looked straight at the trees and called, 'Zacchaeus! Zacchaeus, come down! I'm eating at your house today.'

'Zacchaeus?' somebody shouted. 'Jesus is eating with Zacchaeus? He's the worst man in town. There must be some mistake!' And everybody moaned and groaned.

Well, almost everybody. One man – one wee little man – climbed down from the tree, as shocked as the rest. Why would someone as good as Jesus want to eat with someone bad like him? But he was happy too. Happier than he'd been for a long, long time. And so, with a smile spreading across his face, Zacchaeus led Jesus to his house.

'What are they saying?' somebody whispered. 'What are they doing in there?' And everybody gathered around the taxman's door.

That's when Zacchaeus threw open his door with a bang!

'Greetings, everyone!' he shouted. 'I have an announcement to make. I've been talking with my new friend, Jesus, and realize that there are a few things I need to change. I've cheated some of you. I admit that. And I want you to know that I'm sorry. So sorry, in fact, that I will pay you back four times more than I stole from you! What's more, I intend to sell half of what I own and give the money to the poor!'

The crowd was shocked. Never, in their whole lives, had they seen anyone change like that! They stood there with their mouths wide open. And nobody said a thing.

Well, almost nobody.

'Don't you see?' said Jesus to the crowd. 'God has sent me to share his love with everybody – even those who have done some very bad things. That's what I have done. And now Zacchaeus loves God too.'

That's when the crowd began to cheer. Jesus. And Zacchaeus. And the whole town of Jericho.

Everybody.

The Great Parade

'Let's go to Jerusalem!' said Jesus to his friends. 'I have something important to do there.'

So they went. And when they could just see the city from a nearby hillside, Jesus said, 'Let's have a parade!'

Jesus' friends were surprised. 'A parade?' they wondered. 'Why a parade?' But no one said anything, because Jesus was already busy giving instructions.

'I want two of you to borrow a donkey,' he said. 'Tell the owner I need it. He'll understand.'

When the two friends returned with the donkey, Jesus hopped on its back, gently nudged its sides, and started down the hill.

His friends followed close behind.

'Hooray for Jesus!' they shouted. 'Jesus is king!'

Down, down, down they rode, towards the city gate.
And the closer they got, the more people joined them.

'It's Jesus the teacher!' someone called.

'It's Jesus the healer!' called someone else.

'Three cheers for Jesus!' called one and all.

Soon there were people everywhere, marching along with the parade and shouting from the roadside.

Some took off their coats and laid them in front of the donkey. Others cut palm branches from the trees and waved them about. There were hundreds, maybe thousands, clapping and dancing and shouting their way through the city gates. Everyone was happy!

Well, almost everyone. Some of the religious leaders didn't like Jesus. They were jealous, because the ordinary people were so fond of him. And when they saw the parade, they frowned.

'Wait just a minute!' they called. 'You can't have a parade here. Tell your friends to be quiet, Jesus.'

But Jesus just laughed. 'Tell them to be quiet? Impossible!' Then he turned to look at the crowd.

'Can't you see?' he said. 'There's so much happiness here that even if I could make the people quiet, the stones in the street would jump up and shout for joy!'

The Widow's Coins

Jesus and his friends went to the Temple. There was a line of people waiting to give their offering. They dropped their coins into a hole in the Temple wall, and the coins clattered into a money box below.

'Come and stand by the wall,' said Jesus to his friends. 'I have some sums for you. If you listen closely, you can hear how many coins each person has given. Let's see who gives the most!'

The first person was a merchant. He looked very rich indeed. And as he dropped in the coins, Jesus' friends counted them.

One, two, three.

Four, five, six.

Seven, eight, nine and ten.

'Ten coins!' said one of Jesus' friends. 'Not bad, but I bet someone will do better.'

And soon someone did. The next man was a lawyer. He was dressed even better than the merchant. And Jesus' friends had to count more quickly as the coins went clattering down.

Two, four, six.

Eight, ten, twelve.

Fourteen, sixteen, eighteen and twenty.

'Twenty coins!' said another of Jesus' friends. 'Twice as many as the first man!'

And then a third man walked up to the money box. He was the richest of them all – and one of the religious leaders.

'Watch out for this one,' Jesus whispered. 'The religious leaders like to send their coins rattling into the hole just as loudly as they can – so that

people will be impressed with what they give.'

And sure enough, that's exactly what he did. The religious leader reached into his money bag and scooped up a handful of coins. He looked around, making sure everyone could see, and poured the coins into the hole with a flourish. They rattled down so quickly that Jesus' friends could hardly count them.

Five, ten, fifteen.

Twenty, twenty-five, thirty.

Thirty-five, forty...

'We give up!' cried Jesus' friends. 'But at least we know the answer to your question. No one is going to give more than that man.' And they turned to walk away.

'Wait just a minute,' said Jesus. 'There's one more person waiting.'

It was an old woman – a widow, dressed in mourning. She pulled two tiny coins out of her purse.

'I wish I could give more,' she whispered. 'But this is all I have.' And she dropped the coins – one, two – into the hole.

Jesus looked at his friends.

'Anybody want to change his answer?' he asked.

'No,' said Jesus' friends. 'The third man gave the most.'

'Really?' Jesus grinned. 'But what about the woman?'

'The woman?' his friends chuckled. 'The woman only put in two coins. We can count, you know.'

'I know,' said Jesus. 'But those were the only two coins she had. The others put in more coins, that's true. But they had plenty more in their pockets and in their money boxes back home. The woman, however, gave everything she had. Don't you see? It all adds up. The woman dropped in the fewest coins, but in the end she gave the most of all!'

An Important Meal

Jesus and his twelve friends sat down to eat. There was lamb and bread and wine. A nice meal. But Jesus was sad.

'What's the matter, Jesus?' asked one of his friends.

'I have to go away tomorrow,' Jesus sighed. 'And I will miss you very much.'

Jesus' friends were surprised. 'Where are you going?' they asked.

'I am going to be with my Father in heaven,' he whispered. 'I am going to die.'

Now Jesus' friends were sad too.

'There are people here in Jerusalem who do not like me,' Jesus explained. 'They do not agree with what I teach. They do not believe I come from God. And tomorrow they will arrest me and hurt me and nail me to a cross and kill me.'

'No!' said Jesus' friends. 'They will not do that. We will not let them!'

Jesus looked at them sadly. 'One of you has already taken money from them and agreed to help them catch me.'

Jesus' friends stared at each other.

'Well, it's not me!' said one.

'It's not me,' said another.

But one of them – a man named Judas – just looked at Jesus, then stood up and walked out of the room.

'Let him go,' Jesus told the others. 'We have something more important to do.'

And with that, Jesus took a chunk of bread and said a thank-you prayer.

'I will never forget you,' he said to his friends. 'And I don't want you to forget me either.' Then he broke the bread in half and passed it round. 'This is my body,' he said. 'I give it up for you. Take it and eat it and remember me.'

Then he took a cup of wine and said a thank-you prayer for that as well.

'This is my blood,' he said. 'God will use it to wash away all the bad things anyone has ever done. Take it and drink it and remember me.'

Then Jesus and his friends sang a goodbye song and walked out together into the night.

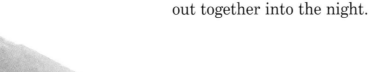

137

A Dreadful Day

When Jesus and his friends had finished their goodbye meal, they walked to a garden to pray. That's where Jesus' enemies found him.

The men had torches and clubs and sticks. They were very frightening. And right in front was Judas, who had been one of Jesus' friends.

Judas crept up to Jesus and kissed him on the cheek. 'This is the man you want!' said Judas. 'Arrest him!' Jesus looked very sad.

Jesus' friends were scared. Most of them ran away. But not Peter. He pulled out a sword and started swinging it about.

'Put your sword away,' said Jesus. 'This is not the time for fighting. I have to go with them. God wants me to.'

So they grabbed Jesus, and dragged him before the religious leaders – the ones who were jealous of him. His trial took all night.

'He says he will destroy our Temple,' said one man.

'He says he is a king,' said another.

'He's a troublemaker!' said one and all.

None of this was true, of course. But it didn't matter, because the leaders had already made up their minds. Jesus was different from them. Jesus wouldn't do what they said. So Jesus would have to die.

They beat Jesus. They hit him hard. Then they took away his clothes, put an old robe round his shoulders and jammed a crown made of thorns on his head. And while the blood ran down his forehead, they called him names and made fun of him. 'So you think you're a king?' they laughed. 'Well, look at you now!'

Jesus never said a word. His body hurt, his heart was breaking, but he never said a word.

They took a cross next, made of heavy wood, and they laid it on his back. 'Move along!' they shouted, and they led him through the city. Some people cried when they saw him. Others cheered. But all of them followed, as he lugged that cross through the city gates and up a nearby hill.

When they got to the top, they laid Jesus on the cross and nailed him to it. It hurt so much. Then they raised the cross, so that everyone could see, and they left him there to die.

A thief, hanging next to him, was afraid. But Jesus talked to him and helped him feel better.

Jesus' mother was there too, standing in the crowd. So Jesus called to one of his friends, 'Take care of her for me, will you, John? She's your mother now.'

But most of the faces in the crowd were not so kind. 'You saved other people,' someone laughed, 'so why can't you save yourself?'

Jesus knew why. It wasn't because his enemies had won. It was because God wanted him there – to take away all the bad things anyone had ever done.

Soon the sky grew dark and the earth shook. It was as if God's own heart was breaking. And then it happened.

'It's done,' Jesus whispered. And in the sadness and the dark, he died.

A Happy Day

It was very early. The birds were still in bed. And the sun had yet to open its bright eye on the world. The sky was grey and grainy. The air was cold. And three women walked slowly towards the graveyard.

Jesus was buried there. And the women were coming to visit his grave.

They talked in sad whispers. They cried. They held each other's hands. Jesus had been dead for three days, and they missed him very much.

Just as they reached the graveyard, however, some surprising things happened. The ground began to shake. The air began to tremble. And, quick as lightning, an angel flashed down from heaven and rolled the stone away from Jesus' tomb!

Everything went quiet. The ground stopped moving. But the women shook with fear.

'Don't be afraid,' the angel said. 'Come and see. The tomb is empty. Jesus is alive!'

Arm in arm, the women crept past the angel and into the tomb. The sheets were still there – the sheets they had wrapped round his dead body. But Jesus himself was gone!

'Where is he?' asked the women. 'What have you done with him?'

'I told you,' smiled the angel. 'He's not dead any more. He's come back to life. And he wants you to tell all his friends.'

The women looked at each other. They didn't know whether to laugh or cry. They could hardly believe it – that is, until they hurried out of the tomb and ran straight into Jesus.

'Oh, Jesus!' they cried. 'It's true. You are alive!' And they fell at his feet, amazed!

'There's no need to be afraid any more,' he said. 'God has made everything all right. But I have a job for you. I want you to tell the rest of my friends that I am alive. Tell them I will meet them on the seashore, in Galilee, where all our adventures started.'

The women waved goodbye and hurried off to Jerusalem. The birds were singing now. The sun's bright eye was wide open. And they had the most amazing story to tell.

On the Road to Emmaus

Talking and walking. Walking and talking.

The two men travelled from Jerusalem to Emmaus.

It was a long journey on foot, and because the two men were followers of Jesus, there was plenty to talk about. Like the rumour that some of his friends had seen him alive again!

So, talking and walking, walking and talking, they made their way.

Then a stranger joined them.

'I hear you talking. I see you walking,' said the stranger. 'You sound excited. What are you talking about?'

'We're talking about Jesus!' said one of the two men.

And then, talking and walking, walking and talking, he explained.

'Jesus was a prophet, sent from God. He did amazing things. Many of us thought he was the Special One God promised, to save us from our enemies.

'But the religious leaders sentenced him to death. The Romans killed him on a cross. And all our hopes died with him.

'That was three days ago. But this morning, some of the women who knew him went to visit his tomb. And his body wasn't there! Better still, an angel told them that Jesus wasn't dead any more. That he was alive again!'

The stranger listened carefully. And then, talking and walking,

walking and talking, he told the two
men what he thought.

'You sound surprised,' he said. 'Isn't that what
the prophets said would happen to the Special One? If this Jesus
died, and came to life again, then surely that shows that he is the Special
One you've been waiting for.'

At last, talking and walking, walking and talking, they came to
Emmaus.

'It's late,' said the two men to the stranger. 'Why don't you stay
here with us overnight?'

And so, talking and walking, walking and talking, they
prepared a simple meal.

'Do you mind if I give thanks for the food?' asked the
stranger.

'Of course not,' said the two men.

So, taking and breaking the bread, the stranger
bowed his head and prayed.

And that's when the two men knew.

The stranger, the man on the road, the one they'd
been talking and walking with all afternoon, wasn't a
stranger at all.

He was Jesus. Alive again!

But before they could say a thing, Jesus disappeared. He
simply wasn't there any more! And they were left alone to
wonder.

'We need to tell someone about this!' they cried.

So they hurried back to Jerusalem.

Not talking. Not walking.

But running and jumping for joy!

Goodbye at Last

When Jesus came back from the dead, he appeared many times and in many different places.

His friends were hiding in a locked room, so the men who killed Jesus couldn't find them. And, all of a sudden, Jesus was there in the room with them! They were frightened. They were confused. They thought he was a ghost!

But Jesus said, 'Don't be afraid. It's me. It really is. Look, here are the marks the nails made in my hands, and the cut the soldier's sword made in my side.'

Then Jesus joined them for dinner and ate a bit of food – to prove that he wasn't a ghost at all.

A few weeks later, his friends were out fishing. They couldn't catch a thing. Then, all of a sudden, they heard a voice from the shore, calling, 'Throw your nets on the other side of the boat!' And when they did, they caught more fish than their boats could hold.

'Wait a minute,' said Peter. 'This is the same thing that happened all those years ago, when Jesus asked us to follow him. It must be him on the beach!' And, all of a sudden, Peter jumped into the sea – clothes and all – and swam back to shore.

The other friends followed as fast as they could and when they arrived, they discovered that Jesus had been doing some fishing of his own. Jesus was cooking fish over a hot fire. They smelled delicious!

'Dry yourselves off. Sit down by the fire,' Jesus said. 'Let's have a picnic right here on the beach.'

A few more weeks passed and, at last, the time came for Jesus to leave – to go to heaven and be with God his Father. So he took one last walk with his friends, up a hill near Lake Galilee where their adventures together had begun.

'I've got to go now,' Jesus said, 'and there is something I want you to do. I will send you a special Helper – God's own Holy Spirit. And with his help, I want you to tell my story to the world. Start in Jerusalem, and don't stop until everybody has the chance to follow me.

'And if you ever feel scared or alone, don't worry. Just talk to me, and I'll be with you. I promise.'

Then, all of a sudden, a cloud wrapped itself round Jesus and carried him into the sky. His friends stood and stared, their mouths open, their eyes filled with tears, until two angels appeared and spoke to them.

'Don't be sad,' the angels said. 'One day, Jesus will come back – in the clouds – just as you've seen him go.'

So off the friends went, down the hill – and into the whole world, to tell the story of Jesus.

The Helper Arrives

Jesus told his friends to wait in Jerusalem – to wait for the Helper he'd promised to send them.

So they waited. They waited and they prayed for forty days. And while they waited, the streets of Jerusalem filled up with people from every land. People from the north and from the south. People from the east and from the west. People from all around the world, who came together to celebrate the Feast of Pentecost.

Jesus' friends were in an upstairs room when suddenly some surprising things began to happen.

They heard a wind blow, harder than the fiercest storm. But nothing was blown about!

They heard the flickering of flames and they watched tongues of fire lick and lap and land on their heads – but nobody smelled any smoke!

And then the Helper came – the Holy Spirit – and he filled them all with the presence and the power of God!

And what they heard next was talking – strange words pouring out of each and every mouth.

So they rushed outside, eager to tell the crowd what had happened. And now, suddenly, everyone could understand. People from the north and from the south. People from the east and from the west. People from all around the world. For now Jesus' friends were able to speak in foreign languages – languages they had never learned – all because of God's Holy Spirit! What better way to tell the world about Jesus?

'So that's what it's all about,' said a man from Spain.

'That's amazing!' said a woman from Africa.

'Tell me again!' asked a man from France.

But there were others who thought Jesus' friends were just talking nonsense.

'These people are drunk!' one man shouted. 'It's nothing but a load of gibberish!'

And that's when Peter stood up.

Peter – who had been with Jesus from the start.

Peter – the fisherman.

Peter – who had never made a speech in his life!

'Listen, everybody!' he shouted. 'We are not filled with wine. We're filled with something else – God's own Holy Spirit!

'Many years ago, a prophet said that this would happen – that God would send his Spirit to help not just special people like prophets and kings, but everyone!

'That has happened to us today. And it has happened because Jesus, who died on a cross, was brought back to life by God himself and now sits beside God in heaven! It was Jesus who sent this wonderful gift to us. Jesus, the Special One we have been waiting for all these years. Jesus, who was put to death by you.'

The people were sorry for what they had done to Jesus.

'What can we do?' they cried.

'Tell God you're sorry,' said Peter. 'Let him wash away all the bad things you have done. And you will receive his Holy Spirit too.'

So that's what the people did. Three thousand of them! They told God they were sorry. They were baptized. And they were filled with God's Holy Spirit.

People from the north and from the south. People from the east and from the west. People from all over the world!

The Beautiful Gate

One afternoon, Peter and John were going to the Temple to pray.

There were lots of ways into the Temple – many different gates. And the gate that Peter and John chose on this particular afternoon was the gate called 'Beautiful'. It was covered all over in bronze and shone brightly in the blazing sun.

Sitting outside the gate, however, was someone who did not feel beautiful at all. He was a poor, sick man who couldn't walk – who had never walked in his whole life. Not ever. And so he sat there, day after day, begging for what little money those passing by would give him.

When Peter and John came near to the man, he reached out his hand.

'Can you spare some change?' he asked, hoping for something beautiful, like a shiny silver or gold coin.

But Peter had something even better in mind.

'I don't have any silver,' he said. 'Or any gold either. But I'll give you what I do have – the power of Jesus at work in me. So by that power, I tell you, stand up! Stand up and walk!'

Then Peter took the man's hand. And right away, he wasn't sick any more. He could feel the power – in his feet and in his ankles and in his legs. So he stood up. He stood up and he started to walk.

And that's not all. He followed Peter and John through the gates into the Temple. And by that time, he wasn't just walking. He was leaping too – walking and leaping and praising God for what had happened to him!

The people saw him and were amazed. And there was only one word for what they saw in his eyes and his face and his dancing feet.

Beautiful.

On the Road to Damascus

Saul did not like Jesus. Not at all.

He had never met Jesus, but he was friendly with the religious leaders who had helped put Jesus to death. And if they said Jesus was bad, that was good enough for him. Saul didn't like the people who followed Jesus either. Not one bit. When they said that Jesus was God's Son, and that he had come back from the dead, it made Saul angry. For he knew that he had tried to do his best for God, and that such things were just not possible.

So when the people who did not like Jesus started throwing stones at Stephen, who was one of Jesus' followers, Saul just stood and watched. He didn't try to stop them. He didn't say, 'That's wrong!' He just held their coats until poor Stephen was dead.

Saul did not like Jesus. Not at all.

So he travelled up and down the country, arresting Jesus' followers, throwing them into prison and putting them to death. The followers of Jesus were afraid, so some of them ran away – far away into other countries. But that did not stop Saul. Not for one minute. When he heard that they had fled to the city of Damascus, he gathered his friends together and set off to arrest them.

Saul did not like Jesus. Not at all.

But Jesus liked Saul. So as Saul hurried along the road to Damascus, Jesus went to meet him! He came to Saul in a vision, with a blinding flash of light so powerful that Saul fell to his knees.

'Saul,' said Jesus. 'Saul, why don't you like me?'

Saul was confused. He had no idea what had happened and who was talking to him. So he asked, 'Who are you?' And when the answer came, Saul trembled with fear.

150

'I am Jesus,' said the voice in the light. 'You've been hurting my friends. And when you do that, you hurt me. Now here's what I want you to do. Get up and go to Damascus, just as you planned. I will send a messenger to tell you what you must do.'

Saul got up, but when he opened his eyes, he could not see! So his friends took him by the hand and led him into Damascus. And there he waited for three days, not eating or drinking a thing.

Meanwhile, Jesus spoke to one of his friends in Damascus – a man named Ananias.

'Ananias,' he said, 'go to Straight Street. A man named Saul is staying there. He's blind, and I want you to heal him.'

'Saul?' cried Ananias. 'But he's the one who's been arresting your followers and putting them to death. He doesn't like you. Not at all!'

'I know,' said Jesus. 'But I like Saul. And I have plans for him. I'm going to send him round the world to tell people everywhere all about me!'

So Ananias went. He laid his hands on Saul and once again, Saul could see. What is more, Saul decided there and then to follow Jesus too. He was baptized, filled with the Holy Spirit, and to show that he was a new person he even took a new name.

'You can call me Paul, from now on,' he said.

And Paul never grew tired of telling people that the man he hadn't liked, liked him anyway, and had given him another chance.

He never grew tired of talking about Jesus. Not at all.

Tabitha Wakes Up

Tabitha sighs.

'Look at all those poor people,' she says to herself as she walks through the streets of Joppa.

So Tabitha tries.

She tries to do something to help them.

'It's what Jesus would have done,' she says to herself as she mends their clothes and makes them new ones.

Then Tabitha dies.

It happens suddenly, and the news races all through the town – up and down the busy streets.

And everyone cries.

They lay her body in an upstairs room, and the people she had helped crowd into the room. They all weep over her and show each other the beautiful things she made for them.

And that's when Peter arrives.

He's one of Jesus' friends. He's been staying in a town nearby, and when the people of Joppa hear, they go to fetch him, hoping that there is something he could do.

So Peter tries.

He tries to do something to help.

'It's what Jesus would have done,' he says to himself as he remembers the time that Jesus brought a dead girl back to life.

'Tabitha, arise!' he says – just like Jesus said to the little girl.

And what a surprise!

Tabitha wakes up, and gets up and goes to greet her friends!

And everyone cries.

Cries all over again. But this time they are tears of joy – and tears of gratitude too. Because their friend is alive again.

The Earth Shakes

The little girl was trapped – taken over by a demon and also by her human masters, who used the powers the demon gave her to make themselves a fortune.

'She'll tell your future!' they shouted to the crowds in Philippi. 'And she'll tell you the meaning of your dreams as well. Just put your money on the table!'

Then Paul and Silas came to town – came to Philippi to tell everyone about Jesus.

And when she saw them, the slave girl shouted, 'These men are the servants of the Most High God.'

Her words were true, but Paul was worried about the poor girl, and worried as well that the crowd would think his message had something to do with the evil power inside her.

So Paul told the demon, 'In the name of Jesus, come out!'

And it left the girl that very second!

That should have been the end of the story. But the girl's two masters could see that she would bring them no money. They were very angry. So they had Paul and Silas beaten and thrown into prison.

Now Paul and Silas were trapped! Their cell door was locked. Their feet were in stocks. They were stuck in a foreign jail.

They might have complained. They might have cursed. But instead they prayed and sang praises to God.

And, almost at once, God answered their prayers.

Shaking and quaking and making much noise, an earthquake broke into their song.

Shaking and quaking and breaking the locks, an earthquake broke open their cell.

And then, shaking and quaking and taking his sword, the jailer went to kill himself. For the law was clear – if the prisoners escaped, he would have to die in their place.

Now the jailer was trapped! And there was no way out but death! Or so he thought.

For that's when Paul shouted: 'Don't hurt yourself! We're all here.'

Shaking and quaking and taking his torch, the jailer went to see. Paul was right. No one had escaped! The jailer fell to his knees.

'I've heard you sing. I've heard you pray. I've seen the saving power of your God. So tell me,' he said to Paul and Silas, 'what must I do to be saved?'

So Paul and Silas told him about Jesus. How he'd died on the cross and come to life again. How this had set everyone free from the power of evil and the fear of death.

The jailer believed what they told him, and he and all his family were baptized.

And now no one – not the girl, not Paul and Silas, not the jailer and his family – was trapped anymore!

Paul is Shipwrecked

City after city. Mile after mile. Year after year.

Paul travelled far and wide, facing danger every day, just so that people could hear about Jesus.

Was Paul worried? Not at all. In every city he visited he left behind a little church. A group of people who wanted to live like Jesus.

But then Paul went to Jerusalem. And that's when he ran into big trouble.

The religious leaders didn't like it when Paul said that Jesus was the Special One that God had promised.

The religious leaders were angry when he said that Jesus really had come back from the dead.

And at last the religious leaders arrested him and beat him.

Some people even wanted to kill Paul, but in the end he was put in chains and sent to Rome to go on trial before the emperor himself.

Was Paul worried? Not at all. He knew that God had said Paul would go to Rome to tell people there about Jesus, and now he was on his way!

Paul was put on a ship with other prisoners and at first the journey went well. But then the wind changed, the ship slowed down, and by the time it reached Crete, it was running late.

Was Paul worried? Not at all. He knew that it wasn't a good time of year to sail, and that if the ship stayed in Crete, everything would be all right. And that's what he told the men in charge. But they didn't want to wait.

So off they sailed, across the choppy sea.

It didn't take long for Paul's warning to come true. A hurricane blew up and the boat was blown like a toy across the water. The sailors did everything they could. They dropped the anchor, they threw the cargo overboard, they held the battered boat together with ropes. But the storm went on and on until all the food had run out and it looked like everyone was going to die.

Was Paul worried? Not at all! He knew God would keep them safe. Calmly, he stood and spoke to the others:

'I had a visit last night – from an angel! He told me that we would get to Rome safely. The ship will be destroyed – run aground on an island, but we will all survive!'

And that's just what happened. The ship was wrecked off the island of Malta. At first the soldiers and sailors thought only of themselves, but Paul convinced the men in charge that the angel's promise would only come true if everyone stuck together. So that's what they did, and everyone was saved!

The people who lived on the island took care of the castaways, and after three months they joined another ship sailing to Rome.

In that big city Paul had to stay in his house until the trial, so while he waited, he told everyone who visited him about Jesus.

Was Paul worried about what would happen to him? Not at all. Instead he was busy – busy writing letters to the churches he had started all over the world. And in one letter he said:

'Don't be worried. Just be thankful and tell God what you need. Jesus will give you the peace of God, and that will help you to face anything!'

Sharing stories with a crowd

Storytelling was never meant to be a one-way street. At its best, it is a kind of dialogue between a storyteller and his listeners. One way to encourage this in a larger group is to give your audience specific ways to participate in the story. Here are my suggestions for how to get groups of children (or adults) more involved in the stories from *The Lion Storyteller Bible*. It's all very simple, although sometimes you may need to spend a while teaching people how to say their lines. The main thing is to have fun with the storytelling and if an idea doesn't work, try something else instead. Enjoy yourself – and your listeners will enjoy themselves too.

In the Beginning (page 8)
Choose people to play Adam, Eve, the sun, the moon and the stars. Adam and Eve lie on the floor, with the sun, moon and stars around them. At the appropriate time, they leap up and act out their parts – a big, bright 'Ta-da!' for the sun, arms in the shape of a crescent for the moon, and 'twinkling' fingers for the stars. Divide the remaining crowd into four groups: the growing things, the flying things, the swimming things and the crawling things. As you tell the story, let them act out their chosen part at the right time.

A Sad Day (page 10)
When you say 'perfect', everyone should say 'AAAH!' – as if they are enjoying a perfect day. When you say 'serpent', they should say 'ssss'. When you say 'guilt' and 'shame', they should say 'OOOH!' – as if they are in pain.

A Special Promise (page 12)
Choose people to be Noah (who says 'OO-ARR' or 'YO-HO-HO' in a deep voice), Noah's wife (who says the same thing in a higher voice), three sons and their wives (who say the same thing, but together), and a dove to fly away (saying 'COO-COO') at the appropriate time. Everybody else plays an animal, making animal sounds at the beginning and when God calls them out of the boat. When it rains, lead the group in a clapping or knee-slapping patter-patter, getting louder each time rain is mentioned. Everyone can sway back and forth while the boat is floating.

The Tall Tower (page 14)
Divide the group into three for the three 'foreign language' sentences at the end.

God's Friend (page 16)
Teach them the phrase 'Abraham trusted God!' to say with you at that point in the story. When Abraham looks up at the stars or down at the ground, the group should look up or down. They can laugh along with Abraham and Sarah too.

The Bad Brother (page 18)
When you say 'Esau', the group needs to say 'HAIRY!' in a big deep voice. When you say 'Jacob', they need to say 'The Cheat!' in a sneaky little voice.

The Runaway (page 20)
When Jacob runs, the group can run on the spot, stamping their feet. When God watches, they should shield their eyes and watch. When Jacob walks, they can walk, stomping their feet slowly.

Joseph the Dreamer (page 22)
Divide the group into two. One half plays Joseph, repeating his lines in the most spoiled and stuck-up way possible. The other group plays the brothers, repeating their lines in the most annoyed (and finally, nasty) way possible.

Joseph the Prisoner (page 24)
When God whispers the meaning of the dreams to Joseph, everybody needs to whisper as well. One half of the group plays the fat cows and gives a big deep 'MOO'. The other half gives a weedy, high-pitched little 'moo' and makes a munching-sound when they devour the fat cows.

Joseph the Ruler (page 26)
The group plays the brothers – bowing down, quaking with fear, and then looking up, grinning and cheering when Joseph forgives them.

The Secret Baby (page 28)
When you say, 'Basket in the water', everyone says 'Splash!' When you say, 'Baby in the basket', everyone says 'Waa'. They say 'Splash!' again when the princess spots the basket, and say 'Waa' again when she sees inside. Then everyone should hide their eyes with Miriam, watch again with God, and jump when God nudges Miriam out.

The Burning Bush (page 30)
Because both snakes and burning things make a 'sss' sound that is the sound you will need everyone to make throughout the story. At the appropriate times, point to the sun and say 'sss', touch your skin and say 'sss', then point straight ahead as if to the bush and say 'sss'. Say 'sss' when the stick turns into a snake, and when Moses picks it up.

The Great Escape (page 32)
This story is one which your listeners can join in by making actions and sounds as you work through the plagues.

A Long Journey (page 34)
Ask the group to repeat the moaning/complaining lines after you in as moaning and complaining a way as possible.

Spies in Canaan (page 36)
Divide the group into two. One side is the moaning and fearful side – repeating the lines of the people and the frightened spies. The other side is Joshua and Caleb and the happy crowd at the end. They can also make sneaky spy motions when the spies creep into the Promised Land.

The Walls Fall Down (page 38)
Divide the audience into three groups: one to the left (the people of Jericho), one on the right (the Israelites), and one in the middle (the wall!), facing the Israelite group. The 'wall' should link arms or do anything to make it more wall-like!

A Brave and Mighty Man (page 40)
Ask everyone to whisper or call 'Gideon!' when God does. Teach a bigger part of the group to pretend to lap the water and a smaller part to scoop it in their hands. Finally, everyone can pretend to blow trumpets, smash pots and shout.

Samson's Great Deeds (page 42)
Whenever you mention that Samson is strong, the group should take a strongman's pose and say 'GRRR'. Then lead them in repeating, 'And his hair just kept on growing', and make long-wavy-hair motions.

Samson and Delilah (page 44)
Everyone can play 'Delilah' and repeat 'Samson, oh, Samson.' You can also use the hair action from the previous story.

Samson and the Philistines (page 46)
Ask everyone to stand and pretend to be the pillars. Lead them in a creaking, then a cracking, then a crumbling sound, swaying more each time. Then they all fall on the floor as the temple collapses.

Ruth Finds a New Home (page 48)

Divide the group into four. Group one say, 'Bye-bye!' with a big wave. Group two say, 'I'm coming with you!' Group three pretend to pick things off the ground and say 'barley, barley, barley, barley… [pause] barley'. Group four say, 'Ooh-la-la!' (after Boaz says he wants to marry Ruth).

Samuel Hears a Voice (page 50)

Ask the group to whisper 'Samuel' with you each time that God calls him. Then they should say, 'Speak, Lord, and I will listen,' with Samuel.

Samuel the Kingmaker (page 52)

Choose nine volunteers: Jesse, David (very small, if possible) and Jesse's seven other sons. Put David at the back and line the others up at the front. Then the rest of the group count with you as Samuel looks for a king. Then Jesse fetches David and brings him to the front.

David the Giant-Killer (page 54)

Choose a small boy or girl to play David. Give them a long sock, folded in two, to swing round their head and let fly. Choose someone a little bigger for King Saul. Sit that person on a chair (throne) in front of the crowd, and drape a large coat or jumper over their shoulders (this can double as armour later and should dwarf little David). Finally, choose someone very big for Goliath (I often go for an adult) and give them something pointed to wave as a spear – a pencil, perhaps!

The Wise King (page 56)

Divide the group into two – one half for each woman. Then ask each group to repeat the appropriate woman's lines after you, facing each other. Roll a jumper into a bundle to be a baby and hold it in your arms while you tell the story.

Elijah and the Ravens (page 58)

Everyone should laugh with Ahab when Elijah tells him the rain will stop, growl with Ahab when he is angry, and flap and 'caw' with the ravens when they come to Elijah's rescue.

A Jar and a Jug (page 60)

Contrast God and Baal as in the previous story. Also, when you say 'Jar', they need to look into a pretend jar and, with amazement, say 'Phwaor!'. When you say 'Jug', they need to pretend to pour something out and go 'Glug!'.

God Sends Fire (page 62)

Do the God/Baal contrast again. Then you should play Elijah and let the group be the prophets of Baal and the people of Israel. They can chant a pretend 'cheer', like 'Baal, Baal, he's no liar. He can set the wood on fire!' Then they should cheer at the end, 'The Lord is God!'

The Helpful Servant (page 64)

The group can join Naaman as he dips himself six times (holding their noses and pretending to dunk themselves), then, on the seventh time, come up, shaking and spluttering.

Jonah the Groaner (page 66)

Ask the audience to groan, softly at first and then louder and louder, every time they hear the phrase 'Jonah groaned'. I always finish with one last 'And what did Jonah do? Jonah groaned!' so the listeners can have a really good groan at the end.

Hezekiah Trusts God (page 68)

Teach the group the three-line number rhyme that appears throughout the story, then lead them in it whenever you reach it, leaving the fourth line for you to say.

Down in the Well (page 70)

Teach everyone the lines, 'Down in the well. Deep down in the well. Deep down in the very bottom of the well.' Do it in a deep voice and emphasize the rhythm. Then lead them in saying the lines whenever they appear.

The Boys Who Liked to Say No (page 72)

Divide the group into three. One group should say a noisy 'No!', the second a high-pitched 'No!', and the third a silly 'No!'. Every time you get to a 'No!' in the story, make it a surprise by pointing to a group at random.

The Men Who Liked to Say No (page 74)

Follow the instructions for the previous story.

Daniel and the Lions (page 76)

Everyone can play the lions. Lead them in growling and baring their teeth, in whimpering away, and in gobbling up their breakfast!

Esther Was a Star (page 78)

Divide the group into three. One group plays Esther and whenever you say 'Esther was a Star', they say 'Ta-da!'. Another group plays the king, and whenever you say he was clueless, they say 'Duh!'. The third group plays Haman, and whenever you mention that he was horrible, they say 'Nyah-ha-ha' in a nasty way.

A Time to Build (page 80)

Divide the group into three. Ask one group to make hammering sounds, another to make sawing sounds and the third to say 'Lovely!'. Do this in sequence every time something is built in the story.

The First Christmas (page 84)

Divide the group into two. Lead one group in shouting 'Good News' and the other in saying 'Bad News' at the appropriate times.

The Wise Men's Visit (page 86)

Divide the group into three – one for each wise man. At the beginning of the story ask each group to repeat the first of their wise man's lines after you. Then you do the rest. For example, when you say, ' "Quick," called the star-watcher to his friends." ' the first group repeats 'Quick!'. And so on with the other groups (wise men).

The Boy in the Temple (page 88)

As you begin, the group should walk slowly on the spot. When Mary and Joseph return to Jerusalem, everyone should turn and walk in the opposite direction. When they find Jesus and go home, they should turn around again to walk.

Jesus is Baptized (page 90)

On each of John's 'shouting' lines, the group should shout the first part of the line after you. So, for example, they shout, 'God is sending someone special!' the first time. And so on.

Jesus' Special Friends (page 92)

The crowd can be fishermen. They can toss the nets into the sea, struggle while the fish pull on the nets, then empty them into the boat.

Down Through the Roof (page 94)

The group can pretend to be Anna with you. Poke your fingers through the hole in a pretend skirt, squeeze through the crowd, look up through the hole in the roof, and try not to giggle (hands over mouths) when Jesus asks his very important question. At the end, look up through the hole in the roof again.

The Centurion's Servant (page 96)

Teach the group the 'Yes sir! Right away, sir!' line, and a salute . You could also divide them into groups, and point to a group at random to keep them on their toes!

The Storm on the Lake (page 98)

Ask the audience as waves to rock back and forth. They need to keep rocking throughout – gently at first and then more wildly as the storm strikes. Then calm them down, as Jesus stills the storm, until they rock gently again.

'Time to Get Up' (page 100)

Choose a girl to lie down at the front and to say 'I'm hungry' when you finally ask her to get up. Divide the rest of the group into three. One group play Jairus, the second group play the woman and the third group play the scornful mourners, all repeating their lines after you.

A Marvellous Picnic (page 102)

Everyone can groan with hunger, then, as the food is shared, they can make a gobbling-up sound. Finally, they can all pat their tummies, get to their feet, wipe pretend crumbs from their mouths and burp.

The Kind Stranger (page 104)

The group to play the people in the crowd, repeating their lines after you. For example, you lead everyone in saying 'Oh no!' when the story text reads: '"Oh no!" the crowd sighed.'

The Two Sisters (page 106)

The group play Martha and repeat the first part of each of her lines ('It's not fair! It's not right! It won't do!') after you.

The Unforgiving Servant (page 108)

Divide the group into two. Lead one half in saying 'I'm really sorry!' to the other half. Then lead the other half in saying 'Hey, that's OK!' back.

'I Can See!' (page 110)

Have the crowd say 'I have a question' with you.

The Two Houses (page 112)

Choose someone to play the rock. They take a wrestler's stance and growl every time you say 'rock'. Choose someone to stand beside them and play the house built on the rock (holding their hands over their head like a roof). Choose someone else to play the other house and the sand. The sand should sway and say 'Shifty, shifty, shifty' every time you say 'sand'. Then choose someone (preferably an adult) to play the rain. Give them a loaded water pistol to spray on the respective pairs when the rain falls. Lead everyone else in being the wind and the waves.

The Big Party (page 114)

Divide the group into three. For the man with land, the first group can shout 'Location! Location! Location!'. The cow people can hold their fingers like horns to their heads and say 'Moo!'. And the wedding people can sing 'Here Comes the Bride!'.

The Good Shepherd (page 116)

Ask everyone to count with you, and then join the shepherd in rejoicing when he finds his sheep. They could also mime looking for the sheep.

The Lost Coin (page 118)

Do the same as in the previous story, with the appropriate lines.

The Big Spender (page 120)

Divide the group into three. Teach the 'younger son' group the line, 'I want my money now!'. Teach the 'father' group the line, 'You are my son!'. And teach the 'older son' group the line, 'It's not fair!'.

Big Bags of Money (page 122)

Make this a kind of maths story. Divide the group into three - one for each servant. The first group should hold up five fingers when the first servant gets his money, then five plus five (if it's a young group, ask them what this adds up to!) when the master returns. Do the same with the other two groups.

The Man Who Came Back (page 124)

Begin by teaching them the little counting rhythm. Then lead the group each time it appears, being sure to slow down when the number stops at nine!

The Pharisee and the Tax Collector (page 126)

Divide the group into two. One group plays the Pharisee, repeating his lines after you. Then do the same with the group playing the tax collector.

Jesus and the Children (page 128)

Choose three big volunteers to stand in front of you like bouncers – arms folded, faces scowling. When you tap them on the shoulder (before each of Jesus' friends delivers his line), they should grunt. Gently push them aside when Jesus chides his friends so at last there's nothing between you and the crowd.

Jesus and the Taxman (page 130)

Choose someone to play Zacchaeus – an adult, preferably. Ask them to climb onto the stage or a chair and to come down as well. Lead everyone else in being the crowd – cheering for the arrival of Jesus, being outraged at his choice of a dinner companion, and then cheering again.

The Great Parade (page 132)

Lead the group in joining the celebration, repeating the crowd's lines. Choose a few to be the religious leaders, repeating their lines. Then lead everyone in a shout of joy at the end.

The Widow's Coins (page 134)

Divide the group into three. Teach one group to count by ones up to ten, the next to count by twos up to twenty and the third to count by fives up to forty.

An Important Meal (page 136)

It might be helpful, given the sombre tone, just to break bread and pour wine and show the group what Jesus did. Choose a few people to join in where the disciples say, 'It's not me!'.

A Dreadful Day (page 138)

Again, because of the sombre tone, the most I would do is to split the group into three, teach them the three lines from the angry witnesses, and ask them to shout those. Otherwise, just tell it with the sadness and gravity it deserves.

A Happy Day (page 140)

Everyone shakes with the earth, trembles with the air and says 'Zoom!' as the angel appears.

The Road to Emmaus (page 142)

Ask the group to walk on the spot and pretend to talk to each other every time you say 'walking and talking'. Take and break the bread yourself when you get there, and then at the end ask everyone to run and jump for joy.

Goodbye at Last (page 144)

Divide the group into four. Teach the first group, 'Don't be afraid. It's me!' (smiling and pointing to yourself). Teach the second group, 'Throw your nets on the other side of the boat' (with a big net-throwing motion). Teach the third group, 'I'll be with you. I promise' (making a cross-your-heart motion). And teach the last group, 'One day, Jesus will come back' (looking up into the sky, eyes shielded).

The Helper Arrives (page 146)

Ask everyone to make 'wind blowing' and 'flame flickering' sounds and movements. Then divide the group into three and teach them these lines. 'Tell me again!' for one group. 'These people are drunk,' for another. And 'What can we do?' for the third.

The Beautiful Gate (page 148)

Ask everyone to say 'beautiful' with you when you get to those parts of the story.

On the Road to Damascus (page 150)

Everyone should say 'Not at all' with you.

Tabitha Wakes Up (page 152)

Teach them the following words and motions. 'Tabitha sighs' – sigh. 'Tabitha tries' – swing your arms in front of your body with a determined expression. 'Tabitha dies' – 'Oh no!'. 'Everyone cries' – 'Boo-hoo-hoo'. 'Peter arrives' – open a door with a 'ta-da!'. 'Peter tries' – do the same as for 'Tabitha tries'. 'Tabitha arise' – raise your arms. 'Surprise' – 'Wow!'. 'Everyone cries' – 'Boo-hoo-hoo' to 'woo-hoo!', for tears of joy!

The Earth Shakes (page 154)

Divide the group into three – one for the girl, one for Paul and Silas, and one for the jailer. When you say 'The girl was trapped', that group should wrap their arms around themselves until she is set free. Do the same with the others. Everyone can stamp their feet for the earthquake.

Paul is Shipwrecked (page 156)

As in 'On the Road to Damascus', ask the group to say the 'Not at all' lines.